YOR

0 3 MAR 2010	2 JUN 2014	
1 1 NOV 2010		
1 7 FEB 2011	0 8 JUN 2017	
	12/6/21	
2 6 JUL 2011		
3 1 MAR 2012		
1 1 APR 2013		

This book should be returned/renewed by
the latest date shown above. Overdue items
incur charges which prevent self-service
renewals. Please contact the library.

Wandsworth Libraries
24 hour Renewal Hotline
01159 293388
www.wandsworth.gov.uk Wandsworth

L.749A (rev.11.2004)

9030 00000 6056 1

Also by Alvin Hall

Money For Life
Winning With Shares
You and Your Money
Your Money or Your Life
Plan Now, Retire Happy

SPEND
LESS,
LIVE
MORE

YOR
11/90

Alvin Hall

HODDER

To Karl Weber, Chappaqua, New York. Thanks for all you, Mary-Jo, and your family have brought to my life in words and in deeds.

This book was originally published under the title
What Not To Spend in 2004 by Hodder & Stoughton
an Hachette UK company.
This updated edition first published in 2009

Copyright © 2004, 2009 by Alvin Hall
Photography © 2004 David Loftus

The right of Alvin Hall to be identified as the Author of
the Work has been asserted by him in accordance with the
Copyright, Designs and Patents Act 1988.

1

All rights reserved. No part of this publication may be
reproduced, stored in a retrieval system, or transmitted, in any
form or by any means without the prior written permission
of the publisher, nor be otherwise circulated in any form of binding
or cover other than that in which it is published and without a
similar condition being imposed on the subsequent purchaser.

A CIP catalogue record for this title is available from the British Library

ISBN 978 1444 70005 3

Designed by Nicky Barneby
Typeset in 12/14pt Eureka by Barneby Ltd, London
Printed and bound by Clays Ltd, St Ives plc

Hodder & Stoughton's policy is to use papers that are
natural, renewable and recyclable products and made
from wood grown in sustainable forests. The logging and
manufacturing processes are expected to conform to the
environmental regulations of the country of origin.

LONDON BOROUGH OF WANDSWORTH	
9030 00000 6056 1	
Askews	29-Oct-2009
332.024 HALL	£7.99
	WWX0005366/0025

ACKNOWLEDGEMENTS

This book is the most collaborative I have ever written. It has been satisfying to see all of the pieces come together, often in ways that were much better than I expected. Creating this kind of book involves lots of effective communication, accommodation, and problem solving among people with differing skills, experiences, and points of view. It is, except in a more condensed form, the same type of communication about your finances and your financial life that I want you, the reader, to have with yourself and with others whose lives are affected by your decisions.

Gill Paul performed the invaluable service of helping me create the overall flow and text of the book. Her diligence and tenacity are truly appreciated.

Karl Weber helped me find my voice and make the right compromises throughout the book, especially where I had to find the balance between providing too little information or too much.

Sarah Pennells helped me keep my fingers on the pulse of change as I was finishing the manuscript.

Richard Atkinson, my editor on this book, managed the entire project expertly, while being nurturing and skilful at handling my perfectionist streak.

David Loftus understood intuitively from the beginning that the pictures had to be evocative and not just illustrative. I like his eye, his sense of humour, his generous and gracious spirit. And he and the make-up artists understood, and laughed at, my deluded desire to look like a young Sydney Poitier.

Thanks to Al Oliver, the art director, Elizabeth Hallett, the production director, Juliet Brightmore, the picture editor, and Nicky Barneby, the book designer, for bringing their experience and brilliant creative eyes to translating my words into images that capture the underlying money-as-lifestyle theme.

Thanks also to my agent, Vicki McIvor, and my publisher, Rowena Webb, for their honesty, instincts, guidance, and friendship. They fulfil my grandmother's advice of always having someone in my life who 'will tell you the truth, whether you like it or not'.

And finally, thanks to all of the people who have written to me asking questions that helped me shape the way the material is presented. Your questions, comments, frustrations, fears, and needs were never far from my mind as I put the words on each page.

CONTENTS

CHAOS THEORY 139

KEEPING YOURSELF AND YOUR MONEY ON TRACK 215

JUGGLING JARGON 237

DIRECTORY 242

INDEX 251

INTRODUCTION

What motivates people to do the right thing with their money? Some say common sense. Some say fear. Others say a hard knock or a swift kick. And the despairing say, shaking their heads, only divine intervention.

I'm more optimistic. I say the best motivator is clear, objective information presented in a way that people can learn one simple step at a time. I believe this because, in addition to presenting television shows, I have taught about the financial markets for over twenty-five years, working with real people, no wiser or cleverer than you, in hundreds of classrooms. I have tried many different ways to help people learn often complex financial information. And there's one method that I've seen work again and again: starting with the basics, then adding new layers of knowledge that evolve naturally out of the previous steps. Each bit of new understanding gives fresh confidence that helps make the next part easier to master. That's the plan of this book.

Starting with the basics doesn't mean dumbing down the information. Some subjects (mortgages and investments come to mind) simply cannot be dumbed down. But I try to avoid the confusing jargon that often makes personal finance seem opaque or impenetrable. I also add serious and funny insights I've gained from my own experiences, as well as those gained from other people I've met on my TV shows, in real life, and from letters I've received.

This book's title, *Spend Less, Live More*, comes from the

recognition that spending is the first thing most of us tend to do when we get our hands on any money – from a new job, a pay rise, a bonus, a gift, the sale of a house, or an inheritance. (I'm no exception.) The sirens of consumerism start calling our names and luring us with promises. They will make us beautiful and sexy. They will provide us with status and prestige. They will confirm our good taste. They will make our lives better, in all ways. Too often we succumb to these enticements.

And then the bill arrives – along with the questions. Was it really worth it? Was it really satisfying? Have our lives really been improved? Probably not.

Spend Less, Live More will help you to pause, to consider what you are about to spend money on, and then make a wise decision: to go ahead if the item of your fancy is one you need and can afford, or to stop if it's a foolish

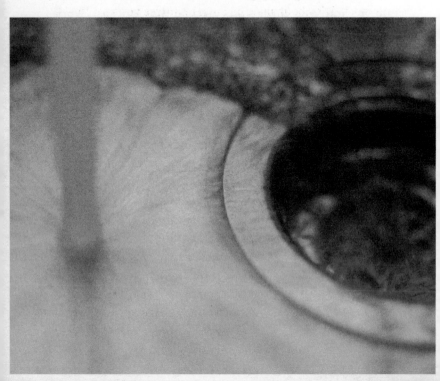

purchase or one you simply can't afford. It will also help you decide what to do with that money once you've resisted temptation. It will cover saving, buying a home, protecting yourself with insurance, building your wealth through investments, and much more.

When it comes to managing money, most people are quick to make excuses. 'I never learned the basics,' they protest. 'It's over my head.' 'I find it so boring.' It's time to put away the excuses. Stop blaming your parents, your siblings, your school, the government, the world, the universe, and life in general. Make yourself responsible for your own financial well-being.

Best of all, *Spend Less, Live More* will make the process fulfilling and fun. It's not about self-denial. It's about discovering the liberation in controlling your financial future. It's about giving yourself choices when you need them most. It's about making smart choices you can live with – not just for an hour or a day, but for a lifetime. You'll soon find that the pleasures of life are far more enjoyable when you know you can afford them!

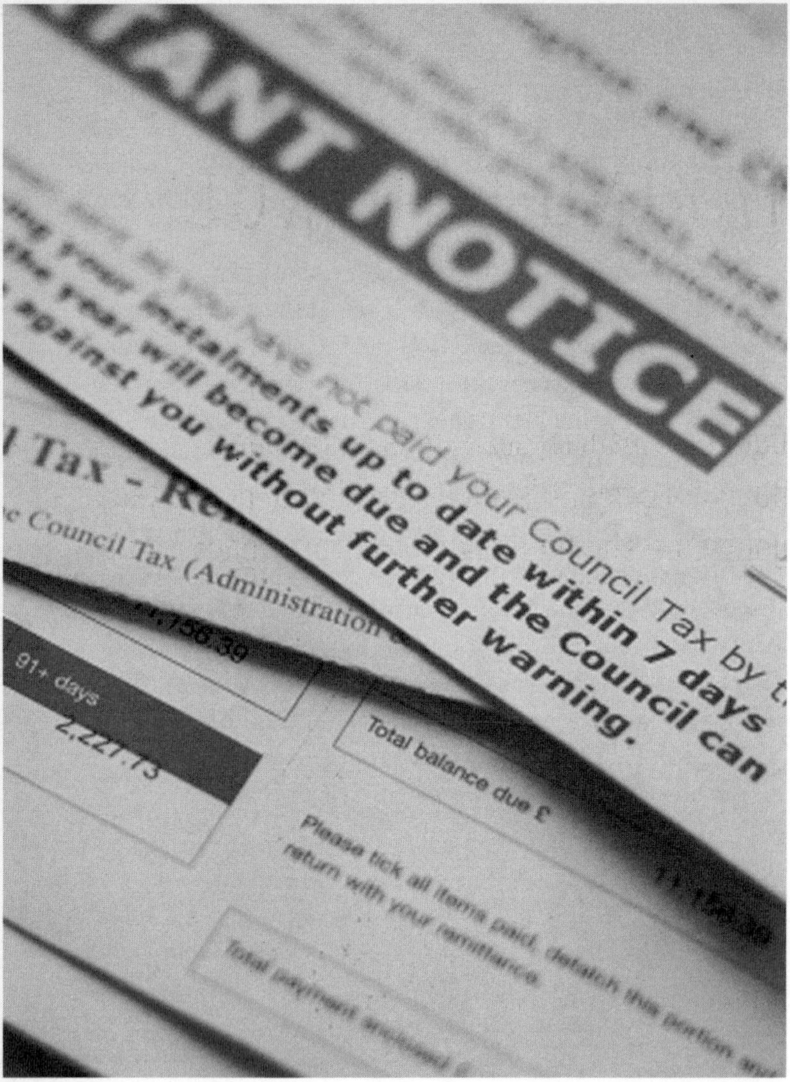
NOTICE
have not paid your Council Tax by
instalments up to date within 7 days
will become due and the Council can
against you without further warning.
Council Tax (Administration
91+ days
2,227.73
Total balance due £
Please tick all items paid,
return with your remittance.

TAKING CONTROL

Building financial security is more than a numbers game. It's about learning to understand yourself – and then taking control of your future.

DEAR DIARY

Do you want to take control of your finances? It's time to confront the realities in black and white. Right now! Take a deep breath and jump in. It might not be as bad as you think – but, of course, there's always a chance it could be worse. And if it is, at least you can start to do something about it.

The first step is to assess your current financial situation. To start, find out exactly where your money is going by keeping a *Spending Diary*. Find a small notebook that will fit in your pocket or handbag. In this notebook, jot down every single thing you spend money on over the next month. Include even the smallest items, like £1 for a newspaper or 35p for a pack of chewing gum. Include purchases you make on debit or credit cards, as well as the monthly bills you pay by cheque or direct debit.

At the end of the month, add up the totals. Figure out how much you spent in every category of expenses: food, clothing, CDs, petrol, movies, cosmetics, what have you. I guarantee you'll get some surprises.

Small expenses have a way of mounting up quickly. If you smoke twenty cigarettes a day, it's costing you around £165 a month. Many people spend even more than this in the pub or on takeaway sandwiches. Lots of us could benefit our waistlines as well as our wallets by cutting back on expensive between-meal snacks. Other items that add up quickly are taxi fares, glossy magazines, and, if you're a parent, those little gifts you buy to keep the kids quiet in supermarkets or newsagents.

Now check to see if there are patterns in your spending. Do you take out a wad of cash on pay-day and fritter it away on non-essentials? Are weekdays or weekends worse for you? Is Friday night on the town your biggest spending splurge? Or is it your lunch hour when you dash to the shops for a bit of a pick-me-up?

No one wants to throw hard-earned money down the drain. Yet most of us do it one way or another. Your Spending Diary is a first step towards identifying your money weaknesses – and measuring what they really cost.

GUIDELINE: To see how money is flowing through your fingers, keep your Spending Diary faithfully for at least a month. Any less won't provide a true picture of your money habits.

TRACKING YOUR MONEY FLOW

Building on your Spending Diary, you're ready to take a broader look at your personal money flow. To do this, you're going to need your bank statements and credit card bills for the last year. You'll also need a calculator. Gather any unpaid bills and the latest statements from your mortgage, savings, and pension providers. (If you can't find statements for the last year, work with what you have – preferably at least six months' worth.)

Fill in the income chart opposite and the spending chart on pages 21–22. You'll need to work out the monthly average for each category. If your earnings vary from month to month, add up last year's total and divide by twelve. If you pay a bill annually, like house insurance, divide the figure by twelve. For bills paid at irregular intervals, add up a year's total and divide by twelve.

If your finances are shared with a partner – a husband, wife, or 'significant other' – this should be a joint exercise. Include income and spending figures for both of you.

Ready? Let's go!

How much do you earn per month?

Salary (take-home)	£ _____
Freelance earnings (after tax)	£ _____
Earnings of partner (take-home)	£ _____
State benefits	£ _____
Pension income	£ _____
Maintenance or child support	£ _____
Investment income	£ _____
Rental income	£ _____
Other income (specify)	£ _____
= TOTAL	£ _____

GUIDELINE: Be complete and honest in tracking your personal money flow. Otherwise, the only person you will be fooling is yourself.

MONTHLY SPENDING CHART

There are two categories here: fixed expenses and discretionary spending. The former includes essential items like mortgage, council tax, and gas. The latter includes costs that you could reduce or even eliminate if you had to.

Fixed Expenses

Home

Rent	£ _____	Medicines, medical costs	£ _____
Electricity	£ _____	Other (specify)	£ _____
Gas	£ _____		

Home

Rent	£ _____
Electricity	£ _____
Gas	£ _____
Water bill	£ _____
Council tax	£ _____
Service charge	£ _____
Buildings insurance	£ _____
Contents insurance	£ _____
Other (specify)	£ _____

Transport

Car loan	£ _____
Petrol	£ _____
Car insurance	£ _____
Road tax	£ _____
Public transport	£ _____
Taxis	£ _____
Other (specify)	£ _____

Daily expenses

Food (at home)	£ _____
Cleaning supplies and toiletries	£ _____
Laundry, dry cleaning	£ _____

Medicines, medical costs	£ _____
Other (specify)	£ _____

Debt repayment

Mortgage	£ _____
Student loans	£ _____
Credit cards	£ _____
Store cards	£ _____
Personal or bank loans	£ _____
Other (specify)	£ _____

Other monthly bills

Telephone (fixed line)	£ _____
Telephone (mobile)	£ _____
Child care	£ _____
Life insurance	£ _____
Income protection insurance	£ _____
Private health insurance	£ _____
Maintenance or child support	£ _____
Pension	£ _____
Endowments	£ _____
Other (specify)	£ _____

= Total Fixed Expenses £ _____

Discretionary Spending

Entertainment

Meals in restaurants,
takeaways £ _____

Pub, off licence,
wine bar £ _____

Tobacco £ _____

TV licence, TV digital
channels fee £ _____

Internet connection £ _____

Books, magazines,
newspapers £ _____

CDs, music and DVDs £ _____

Tickets for cinema,
concerts, sports £ _____

Sports, hobbies, club
memberships £ _____

Kids' activities £ _____

Gambling £ _____

Home decoration,
gardening £ _____

Other (specify) £ _____

Irregular expenses

Home repairs £ _____

Appliances £ _____

Car repairs £ _____

Pets (including
vet bills) £ _____

Holidays, travel £ _____

Christmas,
seasonal gifts £ _____

Birthdays and
non-seasonal gifts £ _____

Clothing £ _____

Toys (for children) £ _____

Hairdresser, barber,
other beauty
treatments £ _____

Other (specify) £ _____

= **Total Discretionary
Spending** £ _____

= **TOTAL SPENDING (Fixed ➕ Discretionary)** £ _____

YOUR BALANCE SHEET

Next, you need to create your *balance sheet* – a simple document that will help you determine your current wealth. The balance sheet has two parts: a list of your current *assets* (what you own) and a list of your current *debts* (what you owe). The difference between the two is your current wealth, or your *net worth*.

Start by listing your assets (see page 24). When estimating the value of the things you own, be realistic. Don't list what you paid for them – estimate what you would get if you had to sell them tomorrow. (It's usually quite a bit less than the amount you paid.) For your home, list your best guess as to its current market value. Don't worry about the amount of money you owe on the mortgage – that will be taken into account later.

Then fill out the list of debts. Here is where your home mortgage debt is included, along with other amounts you may owe.

Once you get a clear picture of your finances, you'll be in a great position to start fixing the areas that aren't working.

Assets

Current value

Cash in current account	£ _____
Cash in savings accounts	£ _____
ISAs	£ _____
Endowment policies	£ _____
Pension schemes	£ _____
Life insurance policy	£ _____
House, flat, or other property	£ _____
Market value of shares, bonds, other investments	£ _____

Market value of possessions:

Car	£ _____
Jewellery	£ _____
Antiques/ collectibles	£ _____
Recreational equipment	£ _____
Any other realizable assets (specify)	£ _____

= Total Assets £ _____

Debts

Balance owed

Home mortgage	£ _____
Second mortgage	£ _____
Student loans	£ _____
Credit cards	£ _____
Store cards	£ _____
Catalogue/mail order debts	£ _____
In-store credit	£ _____
Bank loans	£ _____
Loans from friends or family	£ _____
All other loans	£ _____
All other unpaid bills	£ _____

= Total Debts £ _____

WHAT DO THE NUMBERS TELL YOU?

How healthy is your financial situation? Let's take a close look at the numbers you just compiled to see what they tell you. We'll start with your money flow.

- If your TOTAL SPENDING is more than your TOTAL INCOME, then you have an obvious and immediate problem. You're on a collision course with the Great Unknown. But you already know this, don't you?
- Look at the debt repayment category of spending. If your debt repayments on personal loans, student loans, and consumer debt (credit cards, store cards, in-store credit) amount to more than 20 per cent of your income, you're heading for trouble.
- If your mortgage payments amount to more than 30 per cent of your monthly income, you're heading for trouble.
- If your DISCRETIONARY SPENDING is equal to or greater than your FIXED EXPENSES, then you may be spending too much. (Exception: If there's a special reason why you have low fixed expenses – if, for example, you have paid off your mortgage and are living rent-free, your spending may be all right.)

Now turn to your balance sheet. Your TOTAL ASSETS should be greater than your TOTAL DEBTS. If not, you have a problem.

On my TV show *Your Money or Your Life*, people often get upset when they're confronted with the truth about their financial picture. There may be tears, anger, and sometimes denial. Frequently we have to switch off the cameras until they compose themselves.

If you find yourself confronting an ugly picture, don't despair. There are solutions for even the worst financial troubles. But before you can fix the problem, you need to use a little self-awareness to figure out how you got into this mess in the first place. Otherwise, you may chase the wolf from the door today, only to have him creep back again next week. To get started, use the quiz over the next page to uncover your money personality type.

GUIDELINE: Look hard at the figures you've come up with. Does your pattern of earning and spending reflect the kind of life you want to live? Does it promise a future of financial improvement and growing wealth – or looming trouble?

WHAT IS YOUR MONEY PERSONALITY?

1. How do you manage gift-shopping at Christmas-time?

○ **A** You use a credit card and hope to earn some overtime or get a bonus that will cover your spending.

○ **B** You use a credit card and avoid thinking about how the bills will be paid.

○ **C** You juggle the costs among several credit cards, depending on which ones haven't reached their limits.

○ **D** You consider Christmas a commercial rip-off and buy as few presents as possible.

○ **E** You look for gifts that reflect your relationship with the recipient without being overly expensive.

2. Bad news: you've just been made redundant. After a small pay-out, your wages will stop. What do you do the next morning?

○ **A** You arrange to meet a friend for lunch. After all, why worry? A new job is sure to turn up.

○ **B** You're so upset you can't face anyone, so you spend the day watching TV.

○ **C** You book a holiday. You deserve it after such a shock, and the redundancy money will pay for it.

○ **D** You contact a solicitor about taking legal action against the company. How dare they make you redundant!

○ **E** You update your CV and make phone calls to everyone you know in the industry.

3. Your debts are growing every month. Would you consider bankruptcy as a way out?

- ○ **A** No need to consider it – something will turn up before the situation gets that bad.
- ○ **B** Bankruptcy is one of your biggest fears – it keeps you awake at night.
- ○ **C** You would never be able to live without credit, so you'll avoid bankruptcy at all costs.
- ○ **D** If you had a large debt to dump, of course you would. Why not?
- ○ **E** You'd rather cut back on your spending and work on reducing debt than consider bankruptcy.

4. What are your tactics in a game of Monopoly?

- ○ **A** Opportunistic – you buy every property you land on.
- ○ **B** Defensive – you pray you won't get caught owing money you don't have.
- ○ **C** High-end – you make sure you own the best streets: Oxford Street, Piccadilly, Bond Street, Park Lane, and Mayfair.
- ○ **D** Aggressive – you focus on blocking the other players.
- ○ **E** Flexible – recognizing the role of luck, you simply try to make the best choice each time it's your turn to play.

5. Which of the following statements comes closest to describing your attitude to money?

- ○ **A** No use in worrying about money – things have a way of working themselves out.
- ○ **B** Money is the biggest source of stress in your life.
- ○ **C** You work hard and deserve a few treats at the end of the day.

○ **D** Money flows to the people who know the angles.

○ **E** Money is important and needs attention, but other things matter more to you.

Count up your answers. Did you select more As, Bs, Cs, Ds, or Es? The answer will reveal your money type, as described on the following pages.

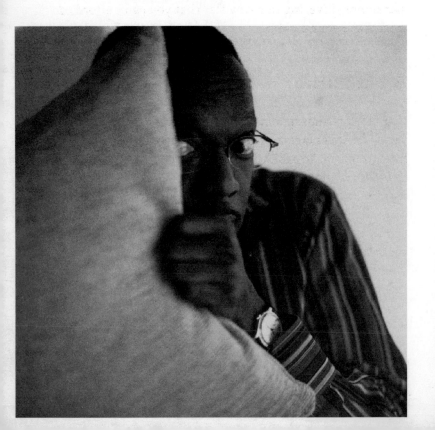

A. The False Optimist

If you answered mainly A, I'm worried about you. Someone's got to worry, because you're not at all concerned yourself. The false optimist is convinced that 'something' will turn up to solve their financial problems. Maybe you're hoping for an inheritance from a rich relative, a stroke of luck in your career, a proposal of marriage from a wealthy admirer, or a winning lottery ticket. Unfortunately, the miracle you're pinning your hopes on is unlikely to happen. You have two options: either take off those rose-tinted glasses and put your financial affairs in order, or plan on a future as an old-age pensioner shivering in a tiny flat that you can't afford to heat. Take your pick!

B. The Ostrich

The ostrich finds money unbearably stressful. Thinking about finances creates a sick knot of fear in the pit of your stomach. To avoid this discomfort, the ostrich develops a range of truth-avoidance excuses: 'I was no good at maths at school.' 'I'm not feeling strong enough at the moment.' 'I have issues with money, it was all my parents' fault.' 'I'm too busy to spend time on my finances right now.' When ostriches get into debt, they avoid taking creditors' phone calls and suffer palpitations when the post drops through the letterbox in the morning. If you're an ostrich, the sooner you start dealing with your problems, the sooner your stress levels will decrease. Flick

ahead to page 231 and read the section on mental freedom. Doesn't that sound nice? All you have to do to achieve it is to follow the advice on the pages between here and there.

C. The Big Spender

If you answered mainly C, you have a touch of the Posh & Becks about you. You are a big spender, though you probably lack the resources needed to support your extravagant fantasies. Why shouldn't you be able to have an expensive haircut or fly to Milan for a personal spend-fest at Dolce & Gabbana or Prada? Why shouldn't you enjoy the most luxurious new sports car or hi-tech, limited-availability sound system? After all, you work hard. Therefore you deserve treats in your life – lots of them. Unfortunately, if your spending is out of control, you'll have to face the consequences sooner or later. Once you learn to regulate your spending, you'll find that treats you save up for and can afford are way more enjoyable than extravagances that push you past your credit limit and cost a fortune in interest.

D. The Hustler

If there's a way to beat the system, you'll try it. The hustler knows every tax dodge in the book, owns (or dreams of owning) a portfolio of 'hot' shares and perhaps a collection of buy-to-let or buy-to-develop properties. You bounce credit card debt from one zero per cent APR card to the next and change mortgage providers at the drop of a percentage point. The problem is that hustlers think of safety nets as a waste of money, so there's nothing to catch them when they fall. And fall they do, because the good times never last forever. Last year's winner is frequently next year's pauper. There are no glamorous shortcuts to financial security, but the system I will outline in this book is much lower risk than the hustler's methods and won't require any energetic ducking and diving.

E. The Balanced Individual

If you answered mainly E, you are a well-balanced individual. You understand that it's necessary to put a certain amount of groundwork into your financial planning. You're unlikely to boast at dinner parties about how well your unit trusts are doing or how much equity you have in your home. Instead, you smile quietly to yourself while the hustlers are bragging about their share deals, the false optimists are describing what they'll do when their windfall arrives, and the big spenders are showing off their latest designer purchases. Read through this book to be sure you're making the most of your assets, and don't skip the section on Chaos Theory, because we all know what can happen to the best-laid plans.

GUIDELINE: Don't expect to find a one-size-fits-all balance. You have to examine yourself – your strengths and your 'little crazinesses' – and find the place between them where you can be responsible.

SEASONAL URGES

Using your Spending Diary, you've identified ways in which your spending varies throughout the month. Now I want you to look at your annual cycles and figure out the trouble spots. Use your bank statements and credit card bills to highlight the peaks and troughs, as well as to look at the kind of things you spend money on. Here are some seasonal urges I've come across:

Spring

The sun comes out and spring/summer clothing collections hit the shops, their bright colours seducing us after the drab greys and browns of winter. The light sparkles through our windows, and we notice areas of the home that look shabby and need a DIY makeover, while the garden bursting into early bloom tempts us to hand over a credit card or two in the garden centre.

Summer

Many people throw caution to the wind when they're on holiday. 'I deserve a good time,' they tell themselves as they rack up hundreds of pounds of debt. 'I'll worry about the bills when I get home.' The July sales tempt us with sexy sunglasses, swimwear, and casual clothes. Perhaps we subconsciously feel that buying them will somehow prolong the hot weather. Sadly, it does not.

Autumn

The children go back to school in early autumn and, although you knew it was coming, you haven't laid any money aside to pay for those new school outfits. This is my personal danger spot in the year, and I don't have children. I was raised in Wakulla County, Florida, in a family with very little money, but somehow my mother made sure that my six brothers and sisters and I had new clothes for starting school. The excitement of this must have lodged in my brain because even now, at the end of August or early September, I really have to watch that I don't overspend. I want something new, warm, and comforting for the chilly weather ahead.

Winter

Christmas is always a difficult time financially. The pressure to buy the best gifts is reinforced by TV, advertising billboards, and store displays. And very few of us are good at sticking to a set budget when such high emotions and temptations are involved. Straight after this, you're bombarded with the January sales and, if you have to fill in a tax return, there is tax to pay at the end of the month. Then along comes Valentine's Day, when you're supposed to show your partner how much you love them by wining and dining, as well as buying flowers, gifts, and cards. 'How much is *your* love worth?' the adverts ask.

GUIDELINE: Identify your own danger period and be cautious when it next comes around. If you know your willpower can be on the wobbly side, leave your credit cards at home.

BE YOUR OWN
FINANCIAL THERAPIST

It's hard not to get emotional when you have money problems. Over the last few years many people have had to confront the fact they've had debts they can't repay, but that doesn't always stop them from having aspirations. Current society sees income as part of identity and people use it to affirm their position in the economic sliding scale of their community. They feel a sense of entitlement – 'I should be able to send my kids to private schools', 'I deserve a bigger house' – and a crashing sense of failure if they can't afford luxuries that those around them seem to be enjoying.

Advertisements and sales techniques emphasize the pressure to acquire possessions so we can demonstrate our 'success' to the world. A salesperson in a fancy store recently said to me, 'I can tell you are a person of exquisite taste,' before wheeling out a gorgeous shearling coat. Was this a sincere compliment? No – it was a flattering sales technique. It was hard for me to overcome this appeal to my vanity, but I'm glad to report that I didn't buy the coat!

One of the biggest jokes advertisers have played on the public is inventing the notion of 'retail therapy'. 'Spending money on yourself will make you feel better' is the subtext in all those commercials where a girl or guy is having a rotten day until they drive along a mountain road in their new car, or try on a new piece of clothing, or spray on that new perfume. That glow won't last long when you see the interest stacking up on your credit card.

I prefer my alternative strategy, which I call restraint therapy. Go out and look but don't buy, and then you can come home feeling good about yourself. Give yourself a 48-hour cooling-off period, to think about whether you really, really need the item that is tempting you. Check your wardrobe to see if you already have something similar, so you don't *need* what you *want* after all. Compare the cost of the item to an essential monthly expense like your mortgage payment. What percentage does it represent and is this a good use of your money? You can also take a long walk, read a magnificent book, or have a chat with a friend instead of spending money.

If you have identified problems in your relationship with money, the solution is to take control. Set a spending budget and stick to it. Write every purchase in a Spending

Diary if you need to boost your self-awareness and self-discipline. If you can't control yourself, you may need professional help to get a grip. There's advice for those with debt problems in the next section.

If your problems are emotional, it might be a good idea to go to a therapist to get to the root of them. Once you become aware of *why* you're overspending, you may be able to act as your own therapist and take responsibility for yourself. The truth is that contrary to the message we get from celebrity magazines, advertisements, and feel-good movies, being able to spend without restraint is not the route to a happy life. The real trick is to manage your money with enough care that you can afford to do what you want to do and be around the people you love.

GUIDELINE: Next time an advertisement catches your eye, look at what it's really saying. More often than not, it will be some variation of the old classic: 'To show the world that you are a success, you must buy X, Y or Z.' How crazy is that?

THE PLAN

If you don't know where you're going, your chances of getting there are only fair. That's why you need a financial road map, with a clear destination, a realistic timetable, and a route to success. And don't forget to plan for bumpy roads and a couple of unexpected detours along the way!

DEVISING YOUR OWN PLAN

In the TV series *Your Money or Your Life*, the most important part of the proceedings takes place behind the scenes. After gathering all financial documents and the initial number crunching, there's the serious analysis to identify problem areas, assess what can be changed, and devise a financial makeover plan. I can't do this for you all individually so you'll have to be your own money doctor, with the help of this book.

Run down the following checklist, answering 'yes', 'no', or 'not sure':

- Are you happy with your overall standard of living?
- Are you happy with where you live? If so, can you afford it?
- Do you pay your credit card bills in full, on time, every month?
- Do you have enough money saved to support yourself for at least four months if you should lose your income?
- Do you have enough life insurance cover to sustain your family's lifestyle if you should die?
- Have you established a set of financial goals for yourself? If so, do you know how you will achieve them?
- Do you have enough of a pension to sustain your standard of living after you retire?
- Do you have a will?
- Do you have any money invested in the stock market (the best way to achieve long-term growth for your cash)?

The questions to which you answered 'no' or 'not sure'

indicate areas in which you need to do some work. Don't worry if they are all 'no's, because I'm going to take you through each area step by step. Even if you answered 'yes' to some or all of the questions, I still recommend that you read each section of the Plan, because you'll find money-saving tips, shortcuts, and warnings highlighted all the way through.

Good luck with creating your personal plan. I'll be with you in spirit!

GUIDELINE: Take the Plan step by step. Don't try to jump ahead of yourself, for example buying shares before you have your savings in place. Think about what would happen if you piled building blocks on a tower that had shaky foundations.

GET OUT OF DEBT

Debt is the single biggest monster lurking in most people's financial cupboard. Consumer debt in the UK averages nearly £4,850 per person, and one in eight confess that they only make the minimum payments on their credit cards every month. That pushes their payment of interest and fees to the maximum, and produces a whole lot of profit for the lenders.

I've got two plans for getting out of debt, depending on the amount you owe. First, get a calculator and follow these steps:

1. Calculate your non-mortgage debt by subtracting your mortgage debt from your total debt (see page 24). (Note: The majority of non-mortgage debt for most people will be unsecured consumer debt, which is not secured against a specific asset like your house.)
   Total Debt – Mortgage Debt = Non-Mortgage Debt

2. Calculate your annual discretionary income. This is your total income (see page 19) minus your fixed expenses (see page 21).
   Total Income – Fixed Expenses = Annual Discretionary Income

3. Divide your non-mortgage debt by your annual discretionary income.
   Non-Mortgage Debt ÷ Annual Discretionary Income = ?

4. Select your Action Plan.
    - If your answer in step 3 is 0.5 or less, follow Plan A below.
    - If your answer in step 3 is greater than 0.5, follow Plan B below.

Plan A

Calculate 10 per cent of your total monthly earnings. Allocate this amount directly to debt repayments (see pages 57–60 for two different methods of making repayments).

Look at pages 21–2 and consider the areas you could cut back to get your spending down to the necessary level. You might be able to do this simply by looking for ways to save on your fixed costs. However, most people will have to cut some discretionary spending.

Here is the good news: if you keep repaying 10 per cent of your earnings per month (and don't add new debt to the old), your debt can be paid off in less than two years.

Plan B

You have a problem. It's time to seek professional help. Start by calling Citizen's Advice and making an appointment. If your debts are pressing and they have a long waiting list in your area, contact the Consumer Credit Counselling Service (CCCS) or National Debtline. You'll find contact details for all of them on page 242.

They are free, confidential services that I recommend highly.

Avoid debt repayment companies that charge you a fee to deal with your creditors directly. The last thing you need at the moment is another expense!

No matter what the level of your debt, don't panic. There's always a way out. The important thing is to start now because the longer you leave it, the more unmanageable it will get.

GUIDELINE: It doesn't make financial sense to have savings (paying a low rate of interest) at the same time as you have debts (charging a high rate). Generally, you should use your savings to pay off your debts. However, if you have no savings at all, it might make sense to keep hold of a small amount, in case you can't borrow money if you have an emergency.

DISCOVERING WAYS TO SAVE

There are many ways to save money, including some that are virtually painless – ways to economize that you'll scarcely notice, except when you see how much healthier your bank balance is looking.

Here are my Top Ten Get-Out-of-Debt Tips. Select the ones that work best for you – or better still, try them all.

1. **Cut your discretionary spending.** Which luxuries can you do without? Could you drop your gym membership and jog in the park instead? Could you eat out less frequently? Or ration yourself when it comes to fashion? Come on, no one *needs* to go to the pub three times a week or buy another pair of black trousers – and perhaps it's time to take your CD or DVD habit in hand!

2. **Look for savings on fixed expenses.** Go through each of your fixed monthly costs and search for better deals on the Internet (or by phone if you aren't online). Despite the credit crunch, it's still possible to switch your mortgage to a better deal (see pages 97-9). Price comparison websites can help you get a better deal with gas and electricity, mobile phone, and insurance, but be aware that you'll often get a different 'best buy' depending on the site you use. There's more information about getting the most from price comparison sites on page 73. The fixed-line and mobile phone industries are fiercely competitive, so take

advantage of the latest price wars. And see pages 73–74 for some ways of saving on your insurance.

3. **Increase your earnings.** When economic times are tough, it might be hard to ask for a pay rise. But sometimes it will be worth a try. If not, consider taking a second job. I did this when I had a problem with credit card debt in my twenties. I took a weekend job as a clerk in a department store and allocated the entire salary to debt repayments. As a result, I got out of debt much quicker than I would have otherwise.

4. **Sell items you no longer need.** You can reduce your debt by cashing in the value in jewellery, antiques, paintings, or collectibles. Work through a reputable dealer (and remember that they'll take commission of around 15 per cent). Have a look at the website www.ebay.co.uk, where you can make good money selling quirky items such as Barbie dolls and accessories, *Star Wars* figures, or rare, limited-edition LPs. And why not set up your own stall at a local car boot sale? You may find some customers who think your old unwanted junk is their lucky find of the day.

5. **Consider subletting a room in your house.** You can earn up to £4,250 a year this way without incurring any tax liabilities. If you take this route, make sure you choose your lodger carefully – remember they'll be living at close quarters with you. I'd recommend you draw up a specific Rent-a-Room (or 'house share') agreement. It sets out house rules and notice period and will state what happens if rental payments are

late. You should also check with your mortgage lender and household insurer before you go ahead.

6. **Consider downsizing your home.** If you own a home that's bigger than you need, you may want to sell it and move to a smaller (and less expensive) place. This is quite a big move, and there will be associated expenses like stamp duty and legal fees. Do your research carefully and make sure you can find somewhere else affordable before you take the plunge. If you are renting your home, look around and see if you can find somewhere cheaper for the time being, until you have climbed out of the hole.

7. **Make sure you're getting all the state benefits and tax breaks you're entitled to.** For example, if you earn less than £13,500 per annum and work at least sixteen hours a week, you could be claiming working tax credit. Housing benefit and council tax reductions are means-tested, so you could be entitled to those as well. Families with a joint household income of less than £58,000, or £66,000 if there is a child less than one year old, can claim child tax credit. Visit the Directgov website (www.direct.gov.uk) for advice and information on tax credits and benefits. It will tell you which government department to claim from. Contact your local council about claims for housing benefit and council tax reductions.

8. **Consider doing without a car, or with only one.** Add up all the costs you listed on pages 21–2, including car loan repayments, petrol, insurance, road tax, MOT

test, maintenance, and parking costs (including tickets). Now find out how much it would cost to use public transport for most of your journeys. Could you save with a monthly (or annual) travel pass? For the journeys that couldn't be made on public transport, how much would a taxi cost? How much would you save per month?

9. **Look for savings through your bank account.** You can get higher interest rates on balances in credit and lower overdraft charges with internet or telephone bank accounts. Check price comparison sites, such as moneyfacts.co.uk (or a newspaper if you're not on-line). Most of these sites list the best deals in current accounts, savings accounts, and credit cards, and you could save a significant amount by switching.

10. **Cut your spending on entertainment.** Choose a budget you can afford and only take a set amount of cash with you next time you go out. Leave the plastic at home, and watch out for the drinking – we all know what alcohol does to willpower. Next time someone says, 'Let's have one more for the road,' just remember that for you this could be another step on the road to the bankruptcy court!

GUIDELINE: Tightening your financial belt can feel a lot like dieting. Will you ever be able to eat pudding again? Yes! Allow enough in your budget for a little treat every month, as a reward for keeping on track. Choose something you enjoy – but only buy it if you've kept within your budget for the month.

PLASTIC SURGERY

No, I don't have any advice to offer about nose jobs or tummy tucks. I've got a different kind of plastic surgery to suggest, one that will save you money rather than cost it. Empty your wallet and lay out all your credit and store cards on the table. Now grab a pair of scissors. Are you feeling nervous?

The truth is you only need two credit cards at most and one debit card. You'll get a better credit score with two *well managed* credit card accounts and if you travel abroad, a second card is useful. And no one needs even a single store card. Not ever.

To decide which credit cards you should get rid of, you need to find out their APRs (annual percentage rates). This is the amount of interest they charge if you don't pay off your bill on time every month. APRs range from zero per cent (for an introductory offer) to 30 per cent for store cards; many credit cards have rates in the vicinity of 16 to 18 per cent. If you don't pay off your card in full, you'll pay interest on the interest that has already accumulated. That means you'll pay more interest than the stated rate would imply. It's scary!

No interest is charged between the date you make the purchase and the date your payment is due so long as you pay off your bill on time every month. This is called the grace period. However, if you take out a cash advance on most credit cards, interest starts accruing straight away. You can be charged additional fees if your payment is even a day late, and further fees if you exceed your credit limit. It's a ridiculously expensive way to borrow money. You can't start building a secure financial future until you've levelled the ground by getting rid of credit card temptation.

Pick up those scissors now and cut up all but two of the cheapest credit cards. (Limit yourself to one if you don't think you have the discipline to handle two.) You'll still have to pay off any debt on them before you can cancel the account, but you've taken a massive first step towards financial well-being by ensuring you can't use them any more.

GUIDELINE: Cut up your excess credit and debit cards into small pieces (or put them in a shredder that takes cards). Dispose of them very carefully – not all the pieces in one place – because identity thieves have been known to sift through rubbish bins (see page 199).

CLEARING DEBT:
THE KNOCKOUT METHOD

Once you've found out the APRs you are paying on all your debts, list your debts in order, beginning with the one that has the highest APR. Your list should look something like this:

Liz's Debts

Company	Total outstanding	Minimum monthly payment	APR
Silly Store Card	£250	£7.50	30%
XYZ Credit Card	£400	£12	25%
Crazy Car Loan	£3,500	£105	18%
Bog-standard Bank Loan	£1,500	£50	8%
= TOTAL DEBT	£5,650		

Work out a level of debt repayment you can afford to make every month. It should be at least one-twenty-fourth (1/24) of the total if you want to clear your debt in two years. In the example above, it should be at least £5,650 ÷ 24 = £235.42. Let's say Liz is repaying £250 a month. Here's how the system works. (Note: The figures used in this example do not take into account the build-up of interest during the period the debt is being paid off.

Interest costs will decrease as debts are paid off and, with diligence, a person should be able to pay off the debt very close to the end of the two-year period.)

- In months one to four, Liz makes only the minimum payments to the bottom three debts (£12 + £105 + £50 = £167), then pays the remaining money to Silly Store Card. That means Liz will pay £250 − £167 = £83 per month to Silly Store Card.
- In month four, Liz will clear Silly Store Card. (Liz may have to use a small amount of month four's payment to pay the remaining balance.) Starting then, she will be able to pay £250 − (£105 + £50) = £95 a month towards XYZ Credit Card.
- By the time Liz has cleared the credit card, around month twenty-one, there will be approximately only £1295 left to pay on the car loan and £450 on the bank loan. She'll make her target of being debt-free in just over two years.

You'll save loads of interest and get out of debt faster by clearing the high-interest debts first while just making minimum payments on the others. There's also the satisfaction of seeing the nastiest debts disappear from the top of the list as you go along. Maybe you'll manage to find a little extra some months just to knock out a high-interest debt that doesn't have much left to repay.

GUIDELINE: Don't miss any of the minimum payments or you'll get hammered with an additional charge. Keep a list in a prominent place and tick off each payment as you make it.

CLEARING DEBT:
THE ROLLOVER METHOD

This method of clearing debts can save you a lot of money in interest payments, but it is not for everyone. The idea is that instead of paying off the debts with the highest rate of interest first, you consolidate your debts into one loan. The advantage is that you pay a lower rate of interest on your debts and you only have one payment to manage every month.

However, the Rollover Method comes with a financial health warning as it's only suitable for certain types of people and, whereas a few years ago it was relatively easy to get a consolidation loan, today there are fewer companies offering them.

The cheapest kind of loan is one that is secured against your home (if you own one).

The downside is that you are borrowing against your future. When you borrow against your home, you run the risk of losing your home if you find you are unable to keep up the payments. Losing your job is one reason why you might not be able to keep up the payments, but there are others. You might have to take a pay cut or work part-time or, if you are married or in a relationship, you might split up. All these changes can put a huge pressure on your budget, and if you have secured more of your debts against your home, you could face the prospect of losing it if you are unable to keep up the repayments.

In the aftermath of the credit crunch, debt advice charities noticed that many of those whose homes were repossessed were not losing their home because of arrears with their main mortgage, but because they could not afford the payments on their secured loan.

There's another problem with consolidating your debts, whether you do so with a secured loan or an ordinary personal loan: you may fall into the trap of becoming complacent and spending over your head *again*. Many people find that the good feeling of getting their debts under control causes them to begin over-indulging and building up a whole new level of unman-ageable debt.

Time and again, I have watched people who've been struggling with debt for years breathe a sigh of relief when their debts are rolled together into one manageable loan. They feel as though a great burden has been lifted off their shoulders; they sleep well for the first time in ages; in fact, they don't feel as though they're in debt any more. Their credit and store cards are clear and beckoning seductively, and I've seen such people run up record-breaking levels of debt all over again in no time at all.

My advice is that you should consider consolidating your debts only if you are prepared to live without any other form of credit for the entire period of the loan. Cut up *all* your credit cards in the meantime. Pay off the loan as fast as you can. Only then should you consider using any other form of credit.

GUIDELINE: Don't consolidate your debts unless you are very disciplined with cast-iron willpower. Be especially cautious before you consolidate your debts into a secured loan. If you are in any doubt, use the Knockout Method on page 57 instead.

GOLDEN RULES OF BORROWING

Debt, especially consumer debt, has a way of draining financial resources and subtly undermining your security. Avoid it as much as possible. However, it's okay to borrow under certain circumstances. For example:

- To renovate your house in a way that adds to its resale value.
- For education, which is an investment in your future earning power.
- If you must have a car for work and can't afford to pay for it in full.
- To cover a medical disaster or other emergency.

Don't borrow to pay for a vacation, holiday gifts, a new wardrobe, or other treats. (No, your desperate desire to get away to Majorca is not an 'emergency'!) And whenever you do borrow, follow these rules:

1. Shop around for the lowest APR. For a short-term loan, you may be able to take advantage of a credit card's zero per cent introductory rate or a zero per cent loan. But read the small print and make sure you pay off the debt before the interest starts building up. If you miss a payment, you may automatically be bumped up to the highest interest rate. Don't fantasize that you can move from one interest-free loan to another; this is becoming less and less possible.

2. For a longer-term loan, you may be charged anything from 7% upwards, depending on how good a credit risk you are. Be aware that you may not get the advertised rate if you're a bad risk.

3. As a general rule, the keener lenders are to give you a loan, the more suspicious you should be; the harder they make it for you, the better the deal is likely to be.

4. Make the highest repayments you can possibly manage so that you clear the debt in the shortest possible time. Most people do the opposite, so they end up paying a lot more in interest. I say: If your monthly repayments don't hurt just a little, they're not high enough.

5. Watch out for early repayment penalties, which are written into the terms of some loans. You should always be able to repay a loan early if you want to, without suffering a financial penalty.

Always read the small print on every contract and ask for written clarification if there's anything you don't understand. If you feel that you were lured unfairly into taking out a loan without the terms being clearly explained, it's worth complaining to the Financial Ombudsman Service (see page 249), the impartial complaints service for the finance industry. The Financial Ombudsman Service can look at complaints about a wide range of companies – including banks and loan providers – if you have a problem.

GUIDELINE: It's a buyer-beware world. Make sure you read everything that you are asked to sign. There are lots of sharks out there, so don't make it easy for them!

A LIQUID SAFETY NET

What would you do if you lost your job? How long would it take you to find another? And how would you survive in the meantime? The recession that followed the credit crunch showed all too clearly that these aren't theoretical questions. No section of the economy is ever safe from a downturn. It just may feel like that when things are going well. You owe it to yourself and to those you love to be prepared for a possible career or financial crisis.

Start by establishing your own safety net. Keep a minimum of four months' salary in a savings account to tide you over. If you are freelance or work in a field where it could be tricky to find the next job, try to keep six months' income on hand instead. (I go even further than this. Like other media professionals I know, I keep a full year's salary in savings. It helps me breathe more easily – and allows me to say 'No' to jobs I really don't want to take without having to wonder where my next meal will come from.)

Keep your savings entirely safe and 'liquid'. Cash in a bank or building society is much safer than money that you have invested (because you don't have the same risk that comes with investing in the stock market). However, as the banking crisis showed, putting your money in a bank or building society is not risk-free.

My advice is to make sure that you are aware of the safety net that exists for savers. In broad terms, the first £50,000 that you have in a bank or building society is protected by a scheme called the Financial Services

Compensation Scheme. However, some banks that have their head office outside the UK are covered by their own country's compensation scheme (although they can 'top up' the protection if it's less than the UK scheme offers). Other banks that share a banking licence are only covered for £50,000 of savings split between the different banks. I recommend that you read about the details of the scheme so you'd know how you would be protected before you open an account (see page 249 for contact details).

If you have money in shares or bonds, those are also classed as 'liquid' because you can sell them straight away. However, you might not get back the full amount you invested, so they should not be classed as a safety net. Property, paintings, and jewellery are 'illiquid' because they can be difficult to sell (i.e. turn into cash) and you may not get their full value if you have to sell them in a hurry.

Your safety net fund should be sacrosanct. This is not a pot for dipping into when you feel like a winter holiday in Mauritius or fancy a new car. If you deplete your savings in a genuine emergency, replace the money as quickly as you can. (I've outlined my favourite savings strategies on pages 65–6.)

You'll be amazed at the peace of mind you enjoy as a result. Having a safety net is one of the key components in your overall financial security, and creating this fund should be done *before* you begin investing for other goals.

GUIDELINE: A savings account that is fully funded and protected by the compensation scheme for savings is a key ingredient of financial security. The account should contain a minimum of three months' salary, but you may want to set yourself higher amounts depending on your situation.

PAY YOURSELF FIRST

One of the most common complaints I hear from people of all financial means is, 'How can I possibly build up a savings account? I'm just barely making ends meet – without saving a penny.'

As with any other life-altering situation, the first step to becoming a saver is to change the way you think. And the most powerful change I can recommend is to adopt the philosophy of *paying yourself first*. Here's how it works.

Imagine you are a company called Joe or Jane Bloggs* Limited (*insert your name here). The company is responsible for various expenses – rent, mortgage, food, transport, and so on. However, on each pay-day, make the company pay *you* first. Set up a direct debit from your current account into your savings account and have the bank transfer the money every pay-day. I suggest earmarking a minimum of 10 per cent of your after-tax income to savings.

If you've been spending every penny you earn, you'll be surprised to find that it's entirely possible to live on 90 per cent of your income with only minor adjustments in your lifestyle. Within a few weeks, you won't even notice the difference. Meanwhile, silently and painlessly, your savings account is growing. At the end of the year, you'll be delighted by the amount you've accumulated.

Here are more of my favourite ways of making saving painless and, dare I say it, even pleasurable.

1. If you have been paying off debts, when you clear the last one start depositing the amount you previously spent on debt repayments into your savings account. You've already proved you can live without this money. Why not carry on doing so?
2. If you get a pay rise at work, allocate the extra take-home pay to savings. You'll never miss what you didn't have before.
3. Add any windfalls, such as inheritances or bonuses, to your savings account. There couldn't be a better use for them than constructing yourself a functional safety net.
4. If you own any shares or bonds that pay dividends, have them paid directly into your savings account. Alternatively, you could also reinvest the dividends, buying more of the same shares.
5. Turn saving into a game of challenges and rewards. For example, suppose you decide you want to save £3,000 this coming year. You could do it by saving £250 a month. The challenge might be to try and save it in eleven months rather than twelve. The reward? Spend the last month's £250 on anything you want.

GUIDELINE: The purpose of savings is to buy yourself peace of mind, especially during difficult times. The safety net will help keep your anxiety and stress levels low.

CHOOSING A NEST FOR YOUR EGG

My grandmother, Rosa L. Hall, was a phenomenal saver, managing to save $20,000 over the years from her very modest income. Her secret? She tucked banknotes inside her bra, creating an ample bosom over her lifetime. Others of her generation, frightened by the bank failures of the 1930s Depression, kept savings in a biscuit tin or tucked under the mattress.

After the turmoil of the last few years, you may feel like doing something similar. However, I wouldn't recommend it. As long as you understand how the safety scheme for savings accounts works, you should be able to make sure your money is covered if a bank or building society fails.

If the bank has its headquarters in the European Economic Area (the countries that make up the EU, plus Norway, Iceland and Lichtenstein), it may belong to its own country's savings compensation scheme. The financial regulator, the Financial Services Authority is looking at reviewing the way the scheme limits work, so make sure you check the rules from time to time (see page 244).

The interest rates paid by banks vary. Check online price comparison sites or the money pages of your weekend newspaper. Be aware that, in the past, some banks offered enticing interest rates that weren't sustainable. So be wary if the rates seem much better than those offered by its rivals.

Having said that, don't shy away of thirty-, sixty- or ninety-day 'lock ins' if they offer better rates than easy access accounts. If you needed your money straight away,

you would just forfeit thirty, sixty or ninety days' interest.

Both interest rates and inflation rates vary from time to time – sometimes quite sharply. As I write, both are low (the Bank of England interest rate is at historically low levels). If you deposit £100 in a savings account that pays 3 per cent, it will grow, in a year's time to £103 – not an enormous growth, but enough to stop inflation from eating away at it.

Whatever the rate you sign up for, the real beauty of

interest lies in the power of *compounding* – that is, the cumulative effect of interest earned on interest. For example, if you maintain the same savings account for a second year, you'll earn interest on the entire £103, which includes both your initial deposit and the first year's interest. At the end of the second year, the money will have grown to £106.09. After year three, the account will be worth £109.27. After year ten, £134.39. And after year thirty, £242.73. (All this is *without* depositing another penny in the account. If you save more money each month – as you should – the entire amount will continuously grow at the same rate.) And if your bank credits the interest to your account every month, then your money will grow faster because the compounding will be occurring every month instead of only at the end of the year, as in the interest example I've used.

Some forms of saving can help you cut your income taxes. A cash Individual Savings Account (ISA), for example, offers instant access to your money and usually a higher rate of interest than ordinary savings accounts and, what's more, all the gains are tax-free. You can put £5,100 a year into a cash ISA from April 2010 (from October 2009 if you're aged 50 or over). National Savings and Investments also has a range of tax-free savings products. You can either get details from NS and I's website or from main post office branches (see page 245 for contact details).

GUIDELINE: Find the account with a competitive interest rate in which to keep your nest egg. Consider internet, telephone and postal accounts, and ISAs, as well as traditional bank or building society accounts, but make sure you are familiar with the rules of the savings compensation scheme.

ARE YOU COVERED?

Insurance isn't considered the most enthralling topic for dinner-party conversation. But surely protecting your future and the future of those you love is worth investing a little time? And if you already have some insurance, you may find you're wasting money on double cover or policies you really don't need. So read on. I'll keep my insurance advice simple and to the point.

Here are the types of insurance you need:

- If you own your home or any other property, you need buildings insurance. (If you have a mortgage, your mortgage provider will insist on it.) Make sure you're covered against any common local problems like flooding or subsidence.
- Everyone should have contents insurance. Walk round your home noting the contents of each room. Estimate the cost to replace each item. Don't forget carpets, electrical items, clothing, and furniture. Add them up to see how much cover you need. If possible, add personal possessions insurance to cover possessions outside the home – for example, a purse or computer that's stolen in an airport.
- If you have a partner and/or children who are dependent on your income, then you need life insurance. How much? Estimate the amount of money your loved ones would need to maintain their lifestyle in your absence, including the cost of raising and educating the kids through university.
- If you are self-employed, or if your employer does not offer generous sick pay entitlement, you need income protection insurance to protect you if you have an accident or get too

sick to work. Statistics show that a large percentage of people are laid up for at least a few months of their lives. (Note: if you are eligible, you may be able to claim the employment and support allowance, which is paid at tiered rates of up to maximum of £95.15 a week.)

- If you own a car, it's illegal to drive without third-party insurance. I advise a minimum of third party, fire, and theft so that you're covered if a stranger joyrides your car into a wall.

Feeling a bit daunted? Perhaps it'll help to consider some of the types of insurance you probably *don't* need:

- If you're satisfied with your current treatment under the NHS, you don't need private medical insurance.
- If you travel to the countries that are part of the European Union (or Norway, Lichtenstein, Iceland or Switzerland) and are only concerned about medical cover, you probably don't need to bother with travel insurance. If you apply for a European Health Insurance Card (or EHIC) online at ehic.org.uk or at your post office, you'll be entitled to free or reduced cost emergency medical treatment. However, it only provides limited cover and you would need travel insurance if you wanted cancellation or baggage cover. Buy an annual policy if you travel regularly.
- Don't buy credit/debit card insurance. You are only liable for the first £50 on each card and are automatically covered for all other charges if a thief uses your card in the EU. (Banks usually waive the £50, so you do not pay anything.) Travel insurance will cover you beyond this initial liability, and you may also have cover through your home contents policy.

- Steer clear of those expensive extended warranties that salespeople urge you to buy to protect your brand-new washing machine or widescreen TV. These are highly profitable to manufacturers because claims are hardly ever made on them.
- Pet insurance may be something you can do without, depending on the type of pet you have and whether you have enough savings you can call on if you need to. If you can cover the cost of vets' bills from your monthly income or savings, you may not need this insurance. But be aware that dog owners can be prosecuted if their pet harms someone or damages their property.

GUIDELINE: Accidents, disability, and death are common occurrences that everyone should be insured against. But don't buy insurance against more far-fetched dangers; instead, save your money and 'self-insure'.

SAVING ON INSURANCE

When you're buying insurance, do as you'd do when buying a TV or a car: shop around. But do make sure that you compare like with like (unless you're happy to reduce or change your cover). Although it is possible to make big savings on insurance, you can also get caught out if you don't check the details.

Here are a few specific ways you can save on your insurance premiums:

- Visit two or three different price comparison sites. Be aware that most sites don't include all the insurance companies that sell policies so you might miss out on the best deal. And some price comparison sites have been criticised for trying to 'cherry pick' the best customers. If you have made a number of claims, you may find it hard to get a quote. You should be able to read the policy document on-line and it is something I recommend that you do (even though it can run to many pages). It is the only way that you can be sure you are getting the right policy for you.
- Compare price quotes from comparison sites with those from a good insurance broker. Make sure your broker is reputable and you are comfortable with them.
- Save on premiums by accepting a higher excess – the amount of each claim you agree to pay. For example, if you have an excess of £500, the policy will be significantly cheaper than one with an excess of £50.
- Some contents insurers will offer discounts if you are in a Neighbourhood Watch scheme. You may also get a discount

if you upgrade your locks or have several claim-free years. (Note: Having a burglar alarm should also reduce your insurance. However, if you claim such a discount and are then burgled when the alarm is not set – even if you are in the garden or on a quick, ten-minute trip to the shops – some insurers won't pay out.)

- Buy *term life* insurance rather than *whole of life*. Term insurance covers you for the period during which your family need you most, such as until the mortgage is paid off and the kids have left home. Whole of life policies are much more expensive and you have to keep paying premiums all your life.

- Income protection insurance premiums will be cheaper if you wait between three and six months after becoming ill before the payments kick in. Premiums will be more expensive if you smoke, work in a hazardous profession, or have pre-existing health complaints. Don't be tempted to lie or you could find the policy doesn't pay out when you need it.

- You can buy car insurance at reduced rates first, if you're over 25, 2nd live in the country and 3rd have off-street parking, a clean driving licence, or a car alarm.

- Remember to cancel policies when you don't need them any more. A man I once helped had an unexplained direct debit from his current account. When I investigated I found that he was still paying contents insurance premiums every month for a property he'd moved out of many years ago.

GUIDELINE: An hour or two spent on the internet or on the phone to a broker getting different insurance quotes could save you hundreds of pounds a year. That's a pretty good return on your time.

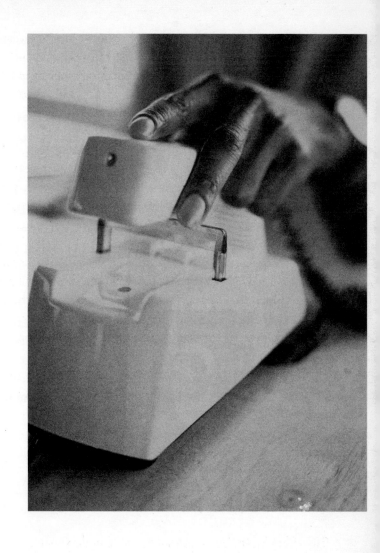

THE FUTURE STARTS HERE

If you've followed the advice laid out in the preceding pages, you will have created an excellent financial foundation. You've identified your main financial challenges, improved your spending habits, cleared your debts, and built a safety net. Now you're ready for the next step in planning your financial future: deciding what you want to do with the rest of your life. After all, money is not a goal in itself, but a means by which you can enjoy life more fully. To plan your finances, you need to know what you want the money for.

It's time to begin setting some personal goals. Where would you like to be living five years from now? Ten years from now? At retirement age? What ambitions do you want to fulfil? What hobbies or talents do you dream of developing? Take some time to fantasize, to dream. Then we'll work together on plans for turning your dreams into reality.

Split your goals into four categories, according to when you'd hope to achieve them. Here are some examples:

Short term (under two years)

Raise the deposit to buy a flat or house; replace that oven with the unpredictable temperature controls; pay for a wonderful wedding day; spend a month trekking in the Himalayas; buy a kiln and learn to make pottery.

Medium term (three to seven years)

Buy a bigger house, or convert the attic of your existing house into an extra room; install a swimming pool in the garden; set up your own business, or retrain for a new career; earn a pilot's licence.

Longer term (eight years plus)

Buy a second home in the country; pay the kids' university tuition fees; take a year off work to travel round the world; buy a yacht and spend all your free time sailing.

Retirement

Emigrate to sunnier climes; return to university and take a degree; buy a top-of-the-range sports car; set up trust funds for your grandchildren.

It's good to dream. Life should be more than a day-in, day-out struggle to pay the bills. The next step is to start putting a price tag on each of your goals.

GUIDELINE: Choose one goal to be achieved in each of the four time periods. Then turn the page to begin planning how you can bring them within reach.

AFFORDING THE LIFE YOU WANT

It will take some research to put a price tag on each of your dreams. But this kind of research will be fun. Let's call it window shopping. Here are some suggestions as to how to figure out realistic cost estimates for your goals:

- To investigate property costs in an area where you'd like to live, talk with estate agents or visit their websites.
- To estimate the cost of a dream holiday, call a few travel agents or cruise the popular travel websites.
- If you dream of a memorable wedding, visit restaurants, dressmakers, and florists. Add up every detail from frocks to food to music.
- Call a swimming pool installation company and get a rough quote.

Whatever your dream, put a price tag on it. Of course, everything will be more expensive in five or ten years, but we'll aim to make your money grow fast enough to outpace inflation, while always keeping in mind your risk tolerance.

The next step is to make a list indicating the total cost of each goal and the number of months until you hope to achieve it (sample opposite). Then divide the cost by the number of months to calculate the amount you need to save each month to make the dream come true.

Goal	Cost	Time Frame	Cost per Month
Deposit for house	£20,000	4 years (48 months)	£416.67
Loft conversion	£12,000	5 years (60 months)	£200.00
2 x university fees (3 years x £3,000 each)	£18,000	15 years (180 months)	£100.00
Year's round-the-world travel for two	£30,000	20 years (240 months)	£125.00

= TOTAL   £841.67

Can you afford to save that amount each month? If not, begin by focusing on your short-term goals. In the example above, it would make sense to concentrate on the house deposit for the first two years. You can start saving for the other goals once you've moved into your home. And, of course, plans can and most likely will change as you go along. Be flexible and make amendments as needed.

Money for short-term goals should be saved in a bank or building society account paying a competitive rate of interest, but remember the rules about keeping your money safe (see page 67). You will get back your money, plus any interest it earns. Shares, on the other hand, could drop in value at the very time that you need access to the money. This investment risk is inappropriate for most people's short-term financial goals.

For medium-term goals, you can invest some money in bonds that mature within the term and some in unit trusts or shares, then keep the rest in liquid form. (I'll explain about buying investment products on pages 113–137.)

For long-term goals, you can build a diversified portfolio of cash, property, stocks, and bonds, including some tax-free investments like ISAs. As the date when you want the money approaches, you will gradually start converting your assets into cash or less risky investments.

For retirement goals, you'll need an adequate pension as well as a diversified portfolio to provide some extra post-retirement income. There's more about pensions on pages 81–91.

GUIDELINE: Look at your monthly spending and consider how much you can afford to save towards your life goals. The sooner you start saving, the quicker you'll achieve your dreams.

WHY YOU MUST HAVE A PENSION

I've heard people offer every excuse in the book for not having a pension plan to secure their retirement. Here are some of the most popular:

- *'I'm too young to worry about a pension.'* Or, alternatively: *'I'm too old and it's too late now.'*

  Both wrong. You can start pension-building at any time in your life, but the sooner you start, the easier it'll be. Here's my handy rule of thumb: divide your current age by two to get the percentage of your take-home salary that you should start investing for retirement now. If you're twenty, then it's just 10 per cent; if you're forty, it's 20 per cent. The older you are when you start, the more aggressive your savings programme must be – but better late than never.

- *'I don't need a private pension – the state will look after me.'*

  Sadly, it won't. At current rates, the basic state pension is £92.95 a week for an individual, £152.30 for a couple. However, you get the full amount only if you have paid enough National Insurance (NI) contributions over the years. (The rules are changing in April 2010 so if you retire after that date you'll only need 30 years of full NI contributions compared to the previous limits of 44 years for men and 39 for women.) Do you think you could live on this money? Wouldn't you *rather* have more?

- *'If I die young, I'll have wasted all that money I contributed to a pension scheme.'*

  Suppose you do die young, do you think you're going to sit fretting in the afterlife about the way you managed your financial affairs? I doubt it. On the other hand, the threat of poverty in old age is very real. You could easily become that old-age pensioner buying your clothes in the Oxfam shop and having to put the cheese back on the supermarket shelf because you can't afford it.

- *'The equity in my property will provide my retirement income.'*

  It's true that a home that grows in value can help contribute to a retirement nest egg. But it's very unlikely that your property will provide enough for you to live on. For one thing, if you sell your property, where will you live? You'll have to buy a smaller or cheaper home, which will eat up at least part of your proceeds. For many people, the amount that remains isn't likely to fund much of a retirement income.

Still not convinced about the importance of a pension? Try doing some voluntary work for a charity like Age Concern and Help the Aged (called Age UK from April 2010). You'll change your mind about pensions quickly.

GUIDELINE: Start a pension scheme in your twenties or thirties to give it time for maximum growth. If you start later, you'll have to save more aggressively to achieve a sum you can live on.

A PENSIONS DECISION TREE

Are you working? —— **YES** —— Do you work for an —— **YES**
employer?

NO

NO

You can contribute up to £3,600 a year to a stakeholder pension (or get someone to do it for you). You could also start your own personal pension scheme or invest in ISAs. Depending on whether you are categorised as a 'carer' you might not build up any entitlement to a state pension. If you are married, make sure your spouse's private or works pension isn't 'single life' but will cover you as well.

If you are self-employed, you can choose from a stakeholder pension, a personal pension scheme, or a self invested personal pension (SIPP). Keep up National Insurance payments to earn your entitlement to a full state pension.

Note. At the time of writing, Personal Accounts are planned to be introduced in 2012. If you are employed you will be automatically enrolled into one of these schemes and your employer will have to make contributions on your behalf and so will you. You can opt out, but unless you can't afford the contributions or you don't like the investment options, you should stay in.

Does your employer offer an occupational pension scheme that you are eligible to join? **YES**—Join your company pension scheme. Your employer will make contributions on your behalf, so it is usually the best way to save for retirement.

NO

Does your employer offer a group personal pension scheme? **YES**—This may have better terms than a personal pension you could arrange on your own, especially if your employer will make contributions on your behalf.

NO

Does your employer offer a stakeholder pension through work? **YES**—If your employer will make contributions to it, it is worth joining their scheme. If not, compare the terms with others you find through your own research.

NO

You will need to make your own retirement income provisions, either with a stakeholder pension, personal pension scheme or a self invested personal pension (SIPP).

A BRAIN TO RELY ON

When you're making big decisions about your financial
future, such as choosing a personal pension or trying to
combine several different investments into a balanced
portfolio, it makes sense to consult a professional financial
adviser. But choosing the right adviser is a challenge in
itself.

First, be clear about the types of adviser available.
Currently there are three different types of adviser,
although that is due to change by 2012. Independent
Financial Advisers (IFAs) can recommend the investment
products of any company. Tied FAs sell only their own
products, and are often paid – at least in part – by
commission. That means they may be under pressure to
sell you something. Multi-tied FAs can sell the products of
a limited number of companies.

Suppose you've decided to consult an IFA. The first
thing to decide is how you will pay them. All IFAs must
now offer you the option of paying an hourly fee, or a
commission. Whichever you choose, the total charges
should be comparable under the current law.

Here are some of the further questions to ask:

- How long have you being doing this job? (*Look for someone
  who's been a financial adviser for at least ten years.*)
- Do you cover all the areas I need advice on? (*Some non-
  specialists do not have enough in-depth knowledge of complex
  areas, like investments and pensions. They should be willing to refer*

you to someone who is more knowledgeable in specific areas or products.)

- What do you consider your greatest successes? (*Listen for attitude here as much as achievement. You're looking for someone who does their homework and keeps up to date on new developments.*)
- Which professional qualifications do you hold? (*As a minimum, financial advisers have to have a certificate in financial planning or its equivalent. A Diploma in financial planning is more advanced and those who have qualified as Certified Financial Planners are fee-charging planners.*)
- How often will there be follow-up meetings to assess progress? Can I call between-times if I have any queries? (*You want an adviser who will be readily available to help you as your needs and financial circumstances change.*)

Also pay close attention to the questions the advisers ask

you. They should ask about the financial products (insurance policies, savings accounts, pensions schemes, investments) you currently own. They should ask about your goals for the future, including the age you want to retire and the post-retirement income you want to live on. They should also try to assess your 'risk tolerance', or how much money you could bear to lose (see page 109). An adviser who fails to ask these questions may be interested in selling a one-size-fits-all financial package that is probably not suitable for you.

Remember, there's no law that says you have to follow your adviser's recommendations. Don't buy any financial product unless you are sure you understand each clause in the contract. You will have grounds for a complaint in the future if they have misled you, but not if you ignored warnings that were there in black and white.

GUIDELINE: Be careful when selecting a financial adviser. You're trusting this person with your financial future – make sure they're worthy of that trust.

SECURING YOUR PENSION

Having a pension is no guarantee of financial security. When media tycoon Robert Maxwell drowned in a fall off his yacht in 1991, he owed the equivalent of twice the national debt of Zimbabwe. In the aftermath, pensioners reliant on Maxwell's Mirror Group faced a gloomy future. Other pensioners have found themselves marooned when the company they'd relied on was wound up (although recent government legislation has introduced an insurance scheme that may help protect such people in future). Still others reach retirement age to find their pension investments are worth far less than they expected because of market swings.

Don't be one of the ones who gets caught in such an unfortunate situation. Monitor your pension annually. If it doesn't look as though it will produce the income you need, start building other savings and investments to compensate. Complicated? Not really. Here's a quick guide to basic pension maths:

1. Look back at your total monthly spending (page 22). How does it compare to the amount you will need to live on in retirement? Think in some detail about how your life will change. Perhaps your mortgage will be paid off by the time you retire. When you stop going to the office, you may be able to spend less on transport and clothing. On the other hand, you may want to spend more on travel or home improvements, and you are likely to need more for medical costs. Based

on these changes, estimate a monthly spending figure for your retirement years. If in doubt, plan on 75 per cent of your current spending.

2. Owing to inflation, £100 worth of goods today will cost more in thirty years' time. Unfortunately, no one knows exactly what the rate of inflation will be between now and the day you retire. As of this writing, inflation is only 3 per cent per year, but this is very low by historic standards and unlikely to persist. If you assume an average inflation rate of 4 per cent, you will need to multiply your monthly budget by 1.48 if you plan to retire in ten years, by 2.19 if you will retire in twenty years, and by 3.24 for retirement in thirty years. The FSA website has a pension calculator that will help. You can access it directly at www.moneymadeclear.fsa.gov.uk.

3. All UK residents are entitled to some level of state pension. For a forecast of the payments you can expect, contact the Future Pension Centre (see page 243) and request form BR19.

4. If you have a company money purchase, personal, or stakeholder pension, you should receive annual statements of the total amount accumulated and an estimate of how much this might grow to and the annual income it may provide at retirement, taking inflation into account. A company with a final salary pension scheme must, at any time you request it, also provide you with any information about your expected pension.

5. Add up your pension income from steps 3 and 4 and compare the total to your estimated retirement

spending. Does your expected income cover your needs? If not, don't despair. You need to boost your saving and investment programme. See how in the pages that follow.

GUIDELINE: Avoid relying on just one private pension scheme; a company collapse could leave you with far less than you expected. A stool with three legs or more is less likely to collapse.

TO RENT OR TO BUY?

'An Englishman's home is his castle,' or so the saying
goes. Unfortunately, I meet all too many young people
who have taken on excessive mortgages to pay for their
castles when they couldn't really afford a single turret.
That's why I'm obliged to debunk the common myth that
everyone should buy a home as soon as possible.

Some defend this myth on what sounds like
common-sense financial grounds. 'Isn't renting like
throwing money down the drain?' they ask. The fact is
that there are distinct advantages to renting, especially
when you are young. You have more flexibility to move
around, escape the headaches of property maintenance,
and avoid locking away most of your cash in a single
investment. Don't think of rent as wasted money. Instead,
consider it simply as another living expense you need to
carry until the time is right for you to buy.

When *should* you buy? Only when you can answer 'Yes'
to each of the following questions.

- Have you paid off your consumer debt and student loans?
- Do you have at least three months' salary in your safety net
  fund and a decent pension scheme?
- Is your job reasonably secure? If you were fired, would your
  liquid savings tide you over until you got another job?
- Have you saved a deposit of at least 10 per cent of the
  property price? (Twenty-five per cent is better still,
  because it will give you access to the best mortgage
  deals.)

- Are you sure that you want to live in the same place for at least three years? (Seven years is the average time spent in a first-time-buyer property. Less than three years and you won't have allowed enough time for the value to grow. And don't forget there are substantial costs to pay every time you buy or sell; see over the page.)

Am I being too cautious? Not really. Just look around you today. There are many people who bought in the summer of 2007 at the height of the property boom who ignored important lessons of the past. When the recession started to bite, thousands had their home repossessed by their bank or building society because they were unable to keep up the mortgage payments. However, it isn't only those who lost their job or had to accept reduced hours who struggled. Many found they could not sell because property prices fell and they were in negative equity. Others were unable to remortgage to a competitive deal because a fall in property prices and a cautious approach from mortgage lenders meant they would not qualify for loans.

Can you now see why I say, 'Don't buy property until you're sure you can afford it'?

GUIDELINE: Don't try to jump on the property ladder before you're ready. Many people have been badly bruised when falling off.

HOW MUCH HOME CAN YOU AFFORD?

When you think you're ready to plunge into the property market, the next step is to determine what you can afford to spend. Do this *before* you begin looking at properties.

Start by calculating the amount of mortgage you can carry. UK mortgage lenders are usually willing to advance up to 3 to 4 times your current salary, or 2.5 to 3 times the combined salaries of a couple. Your credit rating and the amount of debt you already have will usually affect how much you are able to borrow and the interest rate (and whether you can borrow at all if you don't seem like a good risk). Use a mortgage calculator (you can find them on mortgage broker or price comparison sites) to work out how much you would have to pay every month. As a rule of thumb, these should not exceed 30 per cent of your take-home salary.

The first-time home buyer is likely to overlook the many other costs involved in buying a home. Here are some of the most significant.

- Stamp duty. You have to pay the government stamp duty at 1 per cent of the purchase price for properties that cost £125,000 to £250,000 (although the government did raise the threshold to £175,000 temporarily until December 2009). Properties costing between £250,000 and £500,000 attract stamp duty at 3 percent, while those costing over £500,000 incur a 4 per cent stamp duty charge. If, however, you buy in a disadvantaged area, there is zero per cent stamp duty on properties costing up to £150,000.

- Mortgage fees and charges can add up to several thousand pounds. Often – but not always – mortgage deals with the lowest rates have the highest arrangement fees. If you borrow more than 75 per cent of the property's value you may be charged a higher lending charge (HLC), which used to go by the name of mortgage indemnity guarantee (MIG). It typically amounts to 7.5 per cent of the total borrowed in excess of 75 per cent of the property's value. Thus, if you borrow £95,000 against a home purchase valued at £100,000, your MIG could cost £1,500. It's another good reason to hold off on buying until you can afford a larger down payment. Different lenders charge MIG in different ways, so it is important to pay careful attention.
- A property survey costs from £200 to £1,000 and upwards, depending on the size of the property and the type of survey.
- Legal fees will amount to £500–£1,000 or more, depending on the complexity of the case.
- Land registry currently costs anywhere from £150 for a £100,000 property to £700 for a £1 million home.
- Removal costs will vary widely, depending on how much you've got to move and how far it's going.

Finally, once you begin the house-hunting process, remember that even the most persuasive and charming estate agent doesn't have your best interests at heart. He or she is employed by the seller and will earn a commission that is a percentage of the selling price. This is a more powerful motivation.

GUIDELINE: Work out what you can realistically afford to spend on a home, and stick to it. If a bidding war erupts over a property you like, don't get sucked in. Sometimes the best deal is the one you *don't* make.

THE MORTGAGE MAZE

There are several decisions to make when you're mortgage shopping. Some boil down to individual preference, but others have clear financial consequences. Here's a walk-through of the most important questions you'll need to answer.

Question 1: Do I want a mortgage with a fixed interest rate or a variable interest rate?

If you take on a fixed-rate mortgage, the interest rate you pay and the amount of your monthly payments will not change, for the period of the fix – two years, five years, or longer. With a variable-rate mortgage, your payments will change as the Bank of England raises and lowers its interest rates. There are several types of these mortgages from which to choose. A *standard variable-rate mortgage* charges the lender's normal rate when no special deals apply. A *discount variable-rate mortgage* offers a rate that is slightly lower than the lender's standard rate. Neither of these rates is guaranteed to change in line with Bank of England base rates. (Sometimes lenders don't pass on any or all of the changes when interest rates fall.) However, a tracker mortgage will always mirror changes to the Bank of England rate. In general, if you think interest rates are likely to rise in the future, you should probably get a fixed-rate loan. Be aware, however, that this type of mortgage is likely to be more expensive when rates are expected to rise. If you think that interest rates are likely to fall, a variable-rate loan is probably better. It will also depend on whether your budget can comfortably handle any increases in your payments if rates move up.

Question 2: Do I want a repayment or interest-only mortgage?

A repayment mortgage, where you pay some of the capital (the original amount you borrowed) and the interest every month is the only way to guarantee that you will pay off the mortgage at the end of the term. You also have the advantage of seeing the amount you owe shrinking on each mortgage statement. This is my preferred route.

Interest-only mortgages are supplemented by investments, such as ISAs or endowment policies, which are designed to pay off the mortgage debt at the end of the term. However, because they are linked to the stock market, there is no guarantee that they will make enough to pay off your loan.

Question 3: Should I consider an offset or current account mortgage

Offset and current account mortgages are two different products. Offset mortgages let you – as the name implies – offset your savings against your mortgage debt. It means you don't earn interest on money you have in the bank, but you reduce the interest you pay on your home loan. Your savings are easy to access but the main disadvantage is that offset mortgages don't generally offer the most competitive rates.

Products that combine your mortgage with your current and savings accounts can be a good idea, but only for people who are very disciplined at monitoring and controlling their spending. If you can manage that, these mortgages can save you a lot of interest over time. But it can be easy to borrow as fast as you make repayments, which means your balance will not shrink. If you are the type of person who is subject to temptation – and I think you know who you are! – don't even consider this type of mortgage. Some flexible mortgages are not as flexible as they appear. If you are close to borrowing 90% of the property's value and house prices fall, you may find your overpayment pot disappears.

Question 4: Should I use a comparison site or mortgage broker?

An increasing number of people use comparison sites to shop around and they can be a useful way of assessing what type of mortgage deals are available at the time you are looking to buy or remortgage. However, they aren't the same as using a mortgage broker.

A price comparison site won't normally give you advice about your individual situation and won't guide you in the direction of lenders that target the market you're in or those that are, for example, particularly efficient with processing applications (which is useful if you're in a hurry). This is something a good mortgage broker should be able to help you with. Before you sign up with a broker, find out how much he or she will charge for arranging your mortgage. Use the same tips recommended for selecting a financial adviser (pages 86–8).

GUIDELINE: Look carefully at each clause in a possible mortgage deal before you sign on the dotted line. You'll be living with these terms for years to come, and seemingly small differences can add up to thousands of pounds.

THE HOME IMPROVEMENT TRAP

Judging by the hordes of eager customers pushing trolleys round Homebase, B&Q, and similar stores every weekend, it seems as though DIY is the new British national sport. Woodstrip floors, quarry tiles, and cans of turquoise emulsion are loaded into the back of estate cars, while credit cards vibrate and hum with over-use.

There's nothing wrong with wanting to express your taste and create a home you truly love living in. But it's a mistake to get into debt doing so, either by using credit or store cards or by adding a lump sum to your mortgage debt.

As we've already noted, the interest rate charged on most credit cards and store cards is very high, making goods and services purchased with these cards shockingly costly if you don't pay off the balance at the end of the month. As for using a mortgage loan to refurbish the house, this creates two very real dangers. First, if interest rates rise sharply, your monthly payments might become more expensive than you can handle. Second, if property prices fall, you could be stuck with *negative equity* – that is, owing more than your home is worth.

Don't assume that all home improvements will add enough value to your property to cover their costs. Most home projects cost more than they will bring you when your house is sold. For example, the experts estimate that you are likely to recoup just 50 to 60 per cent of the cost of adding a new kitchen or bathroom, 80 per cent of the cost of installing central heating, and some 50 to 75 per cent of the cost of double glazing. Most garden improvements don't increase the selling price of a house by a single penny.

If adding value is your primary motivation, ask local estate agents about the most desirable add-ons. And remember: no matter how much you improve a two-up, two-down terrace in an area full of other such houses, its value will never greatly exceed that of the house next door.

On the other hand, it's definitely worth giving a cosmetic makeover to your house before putting it on the market. A fresh coat of paint, regrouted tiles, perhaps new work surfaces or smart cupboard doors on the kitchen units are all relatively inexpensive and will help make a good first impression on a potential buyer. (See the list of home improvements I do and do not recommend on the opposite page.)

GUIDELINE: If you want to fix up your home for your own enjoyment, go ahead. But don't get over your head in debt to do so. And don't expect to make a profit from your improvements – you probably won't.

THE TOP TEN DO'S AND DON'TS OF DIY AND HOME DECORATION

I'm no home improvement expert; look elsewhere for advice on how to hang a shelf or replace a tap. But the following lists will help you evaluate the *financial* benefits you should expect (or not) from the most popular DIY projects.

Do . . .

- Create off-street parking or add a garage.
- Install a power shower.
- Add central heating, if your house lacks it.
- Paint walls, ceilings, and woodwork in light, unobtrusive colours.
- Replace old-fashioned coloured bathroom suites with simple, good-quality fixtures in white.
- Update Formica kitchens with medium-price-range wooden units; or replace only the work surfaces, drawers, and door fronts if the underlying units are solid.
- Expose wooden floors (if the boards are in good condition), or install neutral fitted carpets or woodstrip flooring.
- Convert a cellar or loft into living or storage space.
- Maximize natural light in the property and take advantage of good views.
- Install an inexpensive, tasteful conservatory in your back garden.

Don't . . .

- Rip out period features, such as cornices, moulding, fireplaces, or tiling.
- Install double glazing that renders windows inoperable.
- Split a room in two, unless the original was enormous.
- Knock two rooms into one bigger one without taking advice from local estate agents.
- Create rooms without windows, or block natural light.
- Carry out a loft conversion with makeshift stairs and ceilings that are too low for you to stand upright.
- Decorate in weird colours and patterns. *Austin Powers: The Movie* is fun; *Austin Powers: The Wallpaper* is not.
- Use woodchip or other textured papers to cover up uneven walls.
- Spend a fortune landscaping your garden and installing a fish pond, fountain, or swimming pool.
- Install stone cladding or UPVC windows (these are definite style no-no's).
- Put your house on the market while paintwork and exterior surfaces look shabby.

GUIDELINE: If you plan to live in your house for ever, then decorate it exactly as you like. If you plan to sell it in the near future, then design it with one eye on mainstream taste to maximize its value.

YOUR PLACE IN THE SUN

When I ask people about their goals in life, I'm surprised how many dream of owning a second home, often in some gloriously sunny climate like Tuscany or the Costa del Sol. It's a lovely dream and one that I'd encourage if you can afford it and plan with care. But if you rush into buying a holiday home without proper forethought, it can become a terrible financial and psychological burden.

First, remember that the purchase price of your second home is only the start of your financial responsibilities. Factor in the cost of a second set of appliances, furniture, crockery, and bedding. And think back to your monthly list of expenditures on your home – then double it. You must be prepared to shoulder all these costs before you buy.

Many people assume they can cover the costs of their holiday home through rental income. Sadly, this rarely happens. Most houses attract guests and holidaymakers only during the main tourist seasons, and it's likely you'll want to occupy the place yourself for part of that time. Thus, you may end up with only one to two months' rent every year. And since the wear and tear on a rental home is phenomenal, you'll have to redecorate and replace basic household items frequently.

Some friends of mine with a property in France once calculated that the four weeks they spent there every year cost them £2,000 a day. For that money, they could have had a five-star holiday in the world's poshest resort!

If you're still intrigued by the thought of owning a

second home abroad, be sure to get legal advice from a local expert – someone who can explain how title deeds are registered in Italy, or the law on getting rid of squatters in Spain.

GUIDELINE: Think long and hard before taking the plunge into buying a second home. Especially avoid making snap decisions while you're on holiday. Come back home, wait for the tan to fade, and think it through before you put down a deposit.

HOW TO PROFIT FROM PROPERTY

After a few years when it seemed that *everyone* could
make money from property, it was a bit of a shock –
to some at least – that property wasn't a one-way bet.
The housing market was rising so sharply that thousands
of people bought a second property, convinced they
could make money. Unfortunately for them, many
were wrong.

Now we're a little wiser. We realise that property isn't a
bad investment, it's just that – like any decision you take
about money – you can't assume that the economic
situation that exists when you invest will last forever.
When mortgages are scarce or expensive and
unemployment rises, property prices will fall –
possibly very sharply.

It is possible to make money from property ownership,
but don't assume it's easy. If you can afford to take a long-
term view and are cautious about how much you borrow,
you may be able to generate a profit. But bear in mind the
following principles:

- Never forget the golden rule: 'Location, location, location'. A
  modest flat on the best street will maintain its value better
  than a palace on the worst street.
- Assume that any rental property will be empty for at least
  two months every year. If you hope to achieve profitability,
  ten months' rent should equal about 140 per cent of your
  annual mortgage payments. In addition, factor in a fall in
  rent and a rise in mortgage rates.

- Always maintain a reserve fund to cover general maintenance and emergency repairs. Plan on cleaning and renovating between tenants or your place will soon look run-down and shabby.
- Be prepared for the hassles of being a landlord: filling out paperwork for leases and taxes, collecting rent, pursuing non-payers, and handling those 4 a.m. calls.
- Quadruple-check your figures before buying to develop, and leave a generous contingency both in money and in time. If you estimate the project will take five months, allow eight. If you think it will cost £20,000, allow at least £30,000. And remember, the extra mortgage interest you must pay during the months before you can sell will come directly off your bottom line.
- When considering a buy-to-let or buy-to-develop property, talk to at least half a dozen estate agents in the area you're considering and base your calculations on their most conservative predictions.

If you're ready for the hard work involved in property ownership, be my guest. Choose well, mortgage conservatively, and you may be able to build up a successful property empire over the years. But don't make the mistake of getting carried away. Even empires fall – sometimes spectacularly.

GUIDELINE: When investing in property, plan and budget for the worst-case scenario. If you do, then any surprises you encounter will be quite tolerable.

WHAT SORT OF
RISK-TAKER ARE YOU?

Every activity in life involves some risk. People die crossing the street or even reaching for a bar of soap in a slippery shower. But those risks are fairly remote, and most of us refuse to let them control our behaviour. (Otherwise, we'd have to spend all day in bed with the curtains drawn to guard against the possibility of sunstroke.) The many rewards of an active life simply can't be enjoyed unless we are willing to incur a modicum of risk.

When it comes to investing, the relationship between risk and reward is especially important. Nearly every investment carries with it some degree of risk. The risks an investor faces vary. There's the risk of losing all or part of the money you invested; there's the risk that your investment gains may fail to keep pace with inflation, which means that your money *loses* value over time; there's even the risk that the investment you choose may gain less than some other investment you *might* have chosen. And experience teaches that the investments with the greatest potential *reward* tend to carry the greatest *risk* as well.

For this reason, it's crucial to consider your own attitude towards risk before embarking on an investment programme. If you are deeply *risk-averse* – that is, if the idea of losing some of your money is almost unbearable – you'll want to choose investments that are relatively low on the risk/reward spectrum. On the other hand, if you

are willing to accept the possibility of loss in the hope of achieving a greater profit, then you may want to consider investments that rank high on the same spectrum.

Imagine I gave you £1,000 to invest for at least five years. Which of these three choices strikes you as most appealing?

1. You can put your money in a savings account where it will earn a guaranteeed 4 per cent a year. The risk that your money will be lost is very low (if you've checked that your savings are covered by the compensation scheme), but you'll never make more than 4 per cent profit a year.
2. You can put the money in an investment fund run by a noted fund manager. During eight of the last ten years, the fund grew by 10 to 18 per cent. But twice during that same time period, the fund *lost* 20 per cent of its value.
3. You can invest the money in a well-known company that is just about to make its stock market debut. Of the last three similar companies to enter the market, two grew in value by 250 per cent in the first few months of trading. But the third went bust, and the investors lost everything.

If you chose option 1, you are probably a *saver* at heart – someone who is most comfortable with low-risk or no-risk money options. Unfortunately, this approach is likely to prevent you from ever enjoying a significant return on your money. You may want to consider taking on a *slightly* greater degree of risk, using investment techniques we'll describe in the pages to come.

If you chose option 2, you are a true *investor* – someone who is willing to take on a real but moderate degree of risk in exchange for significant potential gains. You are probably psychologically prepared for the ups and downs that are inevitable in most investing.

If you chose option 3, you are probably a *speculator* – someone who enjoys the excitement of gambling with their money, and is willing to take on a high degree of risk in the hope of scoring a huge return. This is a dangerous way of life, one that is likely to lead to huge losses, maybe even bankruptcy, in the long run. It's best to speculate on high-risk/high-return investments with only a *small portion* of your money.

GUIDELINE: The higher you climb up the ladder of risk with money, the more you can make and lose. Keep both the potential gains and losses always in clear view. Most people fail to think about the risk of loss, almost always to their detriment.

SNAKES AND LADDERS

We referred before to the *risk/reward* spectrum – a scale along which all investments might be arrayed, from those with the lowest potential risk and reward to those with the highest. Over the page, you'll find one possible version of such a spectrum, indicating in general terms which kinds of investments carry what level of risk and reward. But be careful. Like all generalizations, these must be taken with a grain of salt. For example, 'Mid-cap shares' in two different companies will have somewhat different risk/reward profiles, though both fall at the same point on the spectrum.

- **Spread betting.** (A complicated technique that involves betting on the movement of share prices. Seventy per cent of spread betters lose their money. Better stay away!)
- **Options.** (A contract that gives you the right to buy or sell an investment at a specified price in the future. Depending on whether you are the buyer or seller of the option, potential losses are even *greater* than the sum invested. For very experienced investors only.)
- **New issues.** (Shares of companies newly available on the market. Very hard to predict.)
- **Penny shares.** (Very cheap shares of stock. The occasional winner is buried among hundreds of losers.)
- **Small-cap shares.** (Shares in smaller companies. Some grow fast and earn enormous profits; most don't.)
- **Mid-cap shares.** (Shares in medium-sized companies. A mixture of laggards and high-flyers.)
- **Blue-chip shares.** (Shares in large, well-established companies. Unlikely to grow very fast, but also unlikely to go belly-up.)
- **Actively managed funds.** (A fund manager makes decisions about which shares to buy and sell. A well-run fund is a solid investment choice.)
- **Tracker funds.** (A fund designed to follow the movement of a stock market index. Tends to move up or down along with the market as a whole.)
- **Corporate bonds.** (You lend money to a company and get a specified return. Usually low-risk, provided the company finances are solid.)
- **Gilts or government bonds.** (You lend money to the government for a specified return. Extremely low-risk, since Her Majesty's government is unlikely to go bust.)
- **Cash ISAs and National Savings and Investments' savings certificates.** (Tax-free savings. Savings certificates run for a fixed term, ISAs generally do not.)
- **Cash deposited with banks and building societies.** (Another virtually guaranteed form of savings.)

DESIGNING YOUR OWN INVESTMENT PORTFOLIO

You tailor your wardrobe to suit your taste and your circumstances, with clothes that you feel comfortable in, that you can afford, and that are appropriate for your age and lifestyle. It's roughly the same with an investment portfolio. You need to choose investments that reflect a degree of risk you are comfortable with and that are appropriate for your personal goals.

The most common investments can be broken down into three main categories: cash, bonds, and shares. These have different degrees of risk: cash is virtually risk-free, bonds carry moderate risk, while shares are relatively risky. They also tend to respond to external events in different ways. For example, share prices are influenced by expectation of a company's growth, bond prices are affected by changes in interest rates, while cash earns interest. For most people, an ideal portfolio will include investments from each of the three categories, in different proportions.

One way of calculating how much money you should invest in each category depends on your age. The rule is: the percentage of your money that you should invest in shares is 100 minus your age. Thus, if you are forty, you should put 60 per cent of your money in shares; if you are sixty, just 40 per cent. (The rest would be divided more or less equally between cash and bonds.)

The rationale for this approach is simple. Shares are relatively risky, but they generally grow handsomely in value in the long run. Thus, a younger person with a longer time horizon can afford to ride the ups and downs of the stock market, while an older person, who will need to use the money sooner, will want it to be in safer securities – those with little or no investment risk.

The recent bear market has shown that this formula can be too risky for some older people, especially those approaching retirement. Use this formula as a guideline, not a rule. Do not be afraid to make that percentage zero, if you feel the risk of shares is not for you.

You may want to design your investment portfolio to mirror the life goals you listed on page 77. Here are some examples of portfolio combinations worth considering.

For the young and care-free
5% cash – 10% bonds – 85% shares
Long-term investing for thirty- and forty-somethings
15% cash – 15% bonds – 70% shares
For forty-somethings with a mix of short-, medium-, and long-term goals
10% cash – 35% bonds – 55% shares
For fifty- and sixty-somethings who are nearing retirement
10% cash – 60% bonds – 30% shares

GUIDELINE: Most investors should build a portfolio that includes a range of investments with different risk/reward characteristics. The best proportions depend on your personality, your goals, and where you are in your life cycle.

THE NAME IS BOND ...
CORPORATE BOND

Most people don't know much about bonds. They lack the heady investment appeal of shares, whose price changes can yield great stories of 'killings' made in the market. Nonetheless, boring bonds can be nice, steady counterweights with which to balance the higher risk associated with shares in your portfolio.

Here's how they work. When you buy a bond, you are lending money to the company concerned (in the case of *corporate bonds*) or to the British government (in the case of *gilts*). In return, the company or government (called the issuer of the bond) promises to pay you a fixed rate of interest each year until the bond matures. At maturity, the issuer promises to repay the principal (a.k.a. face value) of the bond to you. It is the steadiness of the income and the return of the bond's face value that makes them attractive. As an investor, you know exactly what you'll make and get back.

Generally, bonds are less risky than shares. But you must not assume they are all risk-free. As with any loan, there's always the chance that the borrower will default – in other words, fail to pay the interest when it is due or to repay the money lent. Gilts are very safe investments. The British government has never defaulted on its interest payments or the repayment of principal. With corporate bonds, the risk of default varies. It is usually less for bonds issued by large, established companies, and greater for bonds issued by smaller, less well established companies. To compensate for the increased risk, such bonds pay a higher interest rate. If the risk of the bonds (as determined by independent ratings agencies) is very high, they are referred to as *junk bonds* or high-yield bonds (a more marketing-friendly term). Be aware that an older company's bonds can also be rated high-yield if the company is experiencing financial problems and is likely to miss its interest payments. High-yield bonds carry a real possibility of loss.

Most people who buy bonds are looking for the highest fixed interest rate they can earn at the lowest possible risk. While investors tend to hold their bonds to maturity, when they are repaid the principal, this does not mean that the market value of bonds stays the same. The market prices of all bonds are affected by changes in interest rates. If interest rates rise, the prices fall. If interest rates fall, the prices rise. Overall, these changes tend to be less volatile than those of stocks, thus when combined with shares in a portfolio, they offset the sometimes rollercoaster-like ride of share prices.

If you are interested in bonds, it is probably best that you learn about the safest type, gilts, first. (I say this because I believe people are more risk-averse with their money than they actually admit to themselves.) The UK Debt Management Office publishes a leaflet explaining how they work. (See page 246 for contact details.) As you become more knowledgeable about and comfortable with the risk associated with bonds, then you can look at higher-interest-paying corporate bonds that may be suitable to your investment needs.

You may have heard of *Premium Bonds*. Don't think of

these as true bonds, but rather as a form of gambling. Each £1 'bond' that you buy goes into a draw every month, where it has a one in 36,000 chance of winning a prize of anything from £25 to £1 million. The odds are better than those of the national lottery, and your money will keep being entered in the draw until you cash in your stake and get it back – without interest. Fun? Yes, for those who like this sort of thing. But don't confuse it with investing.

Bonds belong in almost any investment portfolio. Not only do their prices rise and fall less sharply than those of shares, bonds also tend to hold their value or even rise when shares fall. This makes them a useful counterbalance in your portfolio. And as we've seen, UK government bonds are very low risk, which makes them akin to an interest-bearing form of cash – a good place to put some money that you *can't* afford to lose.

GUIDELINE: When interest rates are low, short-term bonds are generally a prudent choice. When they are high, buy long-term bonds to capture the interest income for the longest period of time.

WHO DO YOU TRUST?

As you've heard, shares are a relatively high-risk, high-return form of investment. Their prices tend to rise and fall significantly, which makes them risky in the short term. But in the long term (over a period of years or decades), shares of good quality, innovative companies tend to rise, so that, historically, these investments have been the best way to make your money grow.

Share investing is also relatively complex. Share values fluctuate depending on the fortunes of the companies they represent, so it's important to understand the business prospects of the firms whose shares you own. For millions of investors who don't have the time or inclination to do the necessary research, a great alternative is to buy into a *unit trust* or *fund*.

A unit trust is a portfolio of investments. In some cases, the investments are chosen by a fund manager who is (or should be) a knowledgeable, expert investor. In other trusts, the investments in the portfolio are not managed; instead they are based on the shares that make up a specific index, like the FTSE (pronounced 'footsie') All Share Index. A unit trust typically holds shares in between 30 and 80 companies, although the number will depend on its own investment objectives and rules. This creates the benefit of *diversification*. Even if an individual company in the trust takes a nose-dive, the others may hold up, thereby preventing the unit trust and its investors from suffering an enormous loss.

There are two basic types of funds: *actively managed funds* and *tracker funds*.

In an actively managed fund, the fund manager constantly researches changes in a company's future prospects as well as changes in the business climate and uses their best judgement to make decisions about when to buy or sell shares. The success of the fund depends in part on the overall fortunes of the economy, in part on the wisdom and insight of the fund manager.

Tracker funds are designed to mirror the progress of *stock market indexes* such as the FTSE All Share Index or the FTSE 350. These indexes are comprised of companies' shares from a wide range of industries. When the overall economy is strong, most of these companies will earn high profits, and their shares will rise in value, making the index rise as well. When the economy flounders, the companies that make up the indexes decline in value, and the index falls.

A tracker fund buys shares in all the companies that make up a given index. Thus, the value of your fund investment will closely mirror changes in the value of the index.

This turns out to be a prudent way to participate in the stock market. In most years, tracker funds usually outperform a majority of actively managed funds – about 80 per cent of them. The fees associated with investing in trackers are also cheaper than those with actively managed funds. So trackers are a good deal all round, frequently providing a better return.

It would be nice to invest in one of the top managed funds that outperform the index – but it's not that easy. Luck is a factor. Quite often a fund that earns a huge return one year loses money the next. If you want to invest in a managed fund, look for one that has performed consistently well for at least five years (these statistics are readily available). Then make sure the same manager is making the investment decisions, because returns could change dramatically if he or she moves on to a new job.

Don't rely on glossy press adverts for your fund performance information. The FSA has tightened the rules on adverts, but copywriters will still put the best gloss on performance. The websites www.morningstar.co.uk and www.trustnet.com compare the performance of different funds, and www.bestinvest.co.uk names the best and worst performers every year.

Put your funds in an Individual Savings Account (ISA), and you won't have any extra tax to pay on your gains. There are strict rules governing the amount of money you can invest annually in an ISA. (The government can change the limits in the future.) For more information, check out the ISA helpline (see page 246).

GUIDELINE: Interested in getting the benefits of share investing, but not sure how to get started? A unit trust or fund can be a great way to put a portion of your money into the stock market without having to master the art of investing in individual company shares on your own.

GETTING STARTED WITH SHARES

Let's say you've got a bit of experience investing. Your financial holdings include a savings account, some bonds, and perhaps a couple of different unit trusts. Now you may feel ready to graduate to the most challenging – and the most potentially rewarding – form of investing: owning individual shares.

Before you proceed, reconsider your level of risk tolerance. If you don't feel ready to take on the risk of buying individual shares, that's fine. Don't do it. The worst mistake any investor can make is to take on more risk than they feel comfortable with. But perhaps you feel able to spare a small amount of money that you could invest in large, established, successful companies, often called *blue chips*. You'll find Britain's leading blue-chip companies listed in the FTSE 100 index in the financial pages of your weekend newspaper. You'll recognize many of the names: Cadbury, Marks & Spencer, Sainsbury, Tesco, Vodafone, and many more. But remember that the share prices of even these companies will move down as well as up as business prospects change. If even the slightest downward movement would bother you, then don't even consider blue chip shares.

If you are comfortable taking on more risk, you could consider riskier shares, such as *mid-caps*. These are medium-sized companies whose values may fluctuate more than blue chips', but which have a good chance of growing rapidly.

Which of the many companies traded on the Stock

Exchange should you invest in? That's a complex decision. One good way to begin is by looking at the industry you work in. Are revenues and profits growing, stagnant, or shrinking? If they are growing, which firms are doing best? Which companies are expanding and which are laying off staff? Which are well run? Which offer the best products?

Now expand your knowledge base by learning about an industry different from the one you work in. The *Financial Times* lists companies according to their *market sector*. Pick one that seems appealing: pharmaceuticals, for example, or media and entertainment, or telecommunication services, or any other. Learn as much as you can about the industry, keeping your eyes and ears open for clues as to which companies are thriving and which are diving. Sometimes these clues may emerge from your own observations. Which of the big supermarket chains have the busiest stores in the best locations in your area? Which of the high-street fashion retailers are all your friends shopping in? What's the consensus in your crowd about the best mobile phone network or the best internet provider?

Social, political, and economic trends may offer clues as to which shares may grow. For example, the average age of the population is rising both in Britain and in most of Europe. Which products and services are likely to grow in popularity as a result? Shopping via the internet is spreading rapidly and has already revolutionized several industries, including book publishing, music, and travel. Which industries might be next? And which companies are poised to benefit?

Of course, searching for clues about the growth potential of industries and companies is only the first step in

successful share investing. You pick up ideas from friends, the media, and your own observations. On the pages that follow, I'll provide additional guidance about how to research the history and future prospects of companies whose shares you are considering.

GUIDELINE: Investing in individual shares can be deeply rewarding. But it's also highly challenging. Begin by learning as much as you can about current trends in the world of business. These trends may contain clues about the most promising companies of the future.

BREAKING THE
STOCK MARKET CODE

Investing in shares is a little like picking horses at the racetrack: you need to develop an eye for winners. And, like the racetrack, the stock market has its own language which many people find arcane. It's important to become familiar with the peculiar jargon of the markets.

Let's start with a sample section of the FTSE index (as printed in the *Financial Times*). These newspaper listings can help you track the daily performance of your shares. But don't worry too much about day-to-day price movements, which can be erratic. It's long-term trends that matter. Here's an explanation of what each of the columns means.

	Company name
Notes	These symbols refer to a key somewhere on the page that give additional explanations about how the figures were calculated
Price	Price per share (in pence)
Chng	Change in share price from previous day
high/low	The highest and lowest values of the share price over the last year
Yld	The yield column tells you the earnings paid per share in the form of a dividend
P/E	P/E is the price to earnings ratio – the share price divided by the earnings per share
Vol	The volume column tells you the number of shares traded the previous day, to the nearest 1,000

The numbers shown in the financial pages provide a foundation for *share analysis* – the art of studying a company's financial prospects in order to determine whether or not it will make a good investment. Further details about a company you are considering can be obtained from your broker, or from www.companyrefs.com.

Share analysis is a complex topic that many people devote a lifetime to, but you don't need that long to get started. Here are some of the basic questions that need to be answered when analysing a potential share investment:

- What industry or industries is the company involved in? How quickly or slowly are those businesses growing? Is the company well positioned to compete in the future?
- How does the company earn a profit? How does its rate of profit compare with other companies in the same industry? Is it growing or declining?
- Is the company's *turnover* (the amount of money it makes before expenses are deducted) growing steadily year-on-year? What are the prospects for future growth?
- Has the company's share price risen fairly steadily over the past several years? How *volatile* is the share price – that is, how large are the price swings from low to high? (If you are risk-averse, avoid volatile shares and stick to those whose growth may be slower but more steady.)
- How does the company's *price to earnings ratio* (P/E ratio) compare with those of its competitors? (A relatively high P/E ratio *may* indicate an overpriced share; a relatively low P/E ratio *may* indicate a bargain.)

- Has the company paid *dividends* (that is, a share of its profits) to investors consistently over the past several years? (This question is important if you want regular income from dividend payments.)
- How much debt is the company carrying? How does this level of debt compare to competing firms? (Excessive debt may forecast financial troubles.)
- After you've done your own homework, read the views of some experts. But take them with a grain of salt. Experts often take the opposite views on the same company!

GUIDELINE: There's no magic formula for picking shares. Start by learning as much as possible about the way a company does business and its history of success (or failure). Once you've identified a firm that is well managed and seems to have strong growth prospects, you may be ready to invest.

CHOOSING AND USING A BROKER

Buying shares isn't quite as simple as buying a blouse or a
TV. You won't get very far by sending a cheque to Unilever
with a note saying, 'Can I have £100-worth of you, please?'
Nor can you walk into your local bank or post office and
buy shares over the counter. Instead, you must use the
services of a *broker*, a kind of middleman (or woman) who
relays your order to a *market maker*, in much the same way
a waiter in a restaurant takes your order to a busy chef.
Therefore, one of the decisions you'll have to make before
you begin share investing is to choose a broker.

There are three different kinds of brokers who offer
three different levels of service:

1. **Execution-only brokers** carry out your orders to buy or
    sell shares without offering any advice or other
    assistance. This is the cheapest service.
2. **Advisory brokers** will help you with research into
    shares, answer your questions about investing, and
    call you with investment ideas you might be
    interested in. The fees charged by advisory brokers
    are higher than those charged by execution-only
    brokers.
3. **Discretionary brokers** invest your money for you.
    This is suitable only for those who don't have the
    time or inclination to manage their own affairs –
    and are willing to trust their financial futures to
    someone else. It's also the most costly form of
    stockbroking service.

If you are an inexperienced investor, I recommend paying a little extra for an advisory broker. To find the right person, ask friends for recommendations or visit a few stockbrokers' offices. Then spend time with the potential broker, asking questions like those we listed for use with any financial adviser (see pages 86–7). You want to find a broker who is patient, open, and willing to answer your questions thoroughly and understandably. The broker should also be focused on your long-term and short-term financial goals and ready to tailor their advice to your own circumstances and objectives.

Once you've chosen a broker, you will normally open a dealing account, in which you'll keep some money on standby. This way, when you want to buy some shares, the transaction can go through without waiting for days for a cheque to clear. You can also leave your share certificates in the name of the stockbroking firm through a nominee account so that they can be sold easily when you want.

Whatever kind of broker you use, buying and selling shares costs money. In addition to your broker's commission on each trade, you have to pay stamp duty of 0.5 per cent on every share purchase and 18 per cent capital gains tax (CGT) on any profits above your annual CGT allowance when you sell. This is one reason why you should *not* buy and sell every time there's a tremor in the market. These transaction costs will eat into your profits.

If you're an experienced investor looking for an execution-only service, you might prefer to use an on-line broker (I've listed some on page 247). These tend to be cheaper than regular brokers.

GUIDELINE: Take the time to find a broker you are comfortable with. And if you find that the broker you choose is discourteous, unreliable, or abrupt, don't hesitate to switch to another firm. You are paying for good service, and deserve to receive it.

MAN THE LIFEBOATS!

Buying the right shares is only half the battle. It's equally important to know when to sell. If you wait until the company's board are issuing a profits warning, the share price will already have sunk before you can speed-dial your broker's number.

I've often been asked what signs investors should have noticed before the collapse of the giant American investment bank Lehman Brothers in 2008 or the British bank Northern Rock in 2007. There were warnings that the good times could not continue, but possibly not at the speed and extent of the downturn. With other examples such as the American energy giant Enron, which failed in 2003, the true situation was cloaked in shadowy accounting practices.

Here's a slightly tongue-in-cheek guide to the warning signs of a company heading for decline. You should be worried if:

- The chief executive seems less concerned about the company's future and more about his pay and perks, especially when these are *not* linked to performance. In the UK, shareholders have led several successful revolts against sky's-the-limit salaries for top executives – a trend I applaud.
- Company managers are selling large blocks of shares in their own company. Perhaps they have good reason to be concerned about the shares' future value.
- The company is either falling behind the times or taking risks that none of its competitors seem to be. The credit crunch showed just how devastating it can be when a

company goes out on a limb. By the same token, refusing to innovate and being stuck in your ways is rarely a winning formula either!

- It's next to impossible to get access to basic information about the company, its products, or its services by phone. If you call and find yourself stuck in telephone hell, unable to speak to a knowledgeable human being, chances are that the company's service and communications systems are in disrepair.
- The company is laying off staff and shutting branch offices – especially when these actions are not part of a comprehensive turnaround plan.

When deciding whether or not to sell shares, don't focus on whether or not you've made a profit. (That will tempt you to hang on to a company that has lost value, hoping against hope for a miraculous recovery.) Forget what you paid for the shares. Step back and ask, 'Knowing what I know about this company, would I now buy these shares at the current price?' If the answer is 'No', then sell.

If you become a regular stock market investor, you'll inevitably suffer some losses. The key to long-term success is to try to learn a lesson from each experience. Did you dabble in an industry you don't know enough about? Were you blinded by hype, rumours, or fads? Or was your investment simply the victim of unforeseeable economic changes, unexpected competition, or sheer bad luck?

GUIDELINE: Focus your share investing on a limited number of companies – no more than ten to twenty firms in several market sectors. Spend a little time each week on reading and research, and periodically re-examine your portfolio to weed out the losers and add some potential winners.

WHAT NOT TO DO: HOW TO GO BROKE WITHOUT REALLY TRYING

We've all made a few foolish financial decisions – I know I have. But to lose everything you own takes either colossal bad luck or a run of truly aggressive foolishness. Sadly, it does happen. Here's a collection of ideas to pursue if you ever want to experience utter poverty – or, if you'd prefer, to avoid prosperity.

1. Sign up for a new pension fund, take out a mortgage, or buy an investment without bothering to read the small print or fully understanding your commitment. Better still, sign on in response to a sales pitch from a stranger on the telephone!
2. If an investment promises to double your money in a year or a 'risk-free' 300 per cent return in five years, buy it straight away. When an offer sounds too good to be true, it probably is. A fool and his money ...
3. Increase your mortgage to the very maximum the lender will allow, and spend your credit cards up to the limit. Then just wait for unexpected expenses, a job loss, or a rise in interest rates. It may take a few months or even a couple of years for this method to ruin you, but be patient – it will.
4. Buy shares according to tips you hear on the golf course or at dinner parties – the kind that come from someone's friend's sister's doctor's cousin who's a secretary at the company concerned.

5. Spend all your waking hours watching the price of your shares, and buy or sell every time they move a few pennies in either direction. Before long, the transaction costs will wipe you out.

6. Answer newspaper adverts or send money to websites that promise you a 'fool-proof' way to make money without even trying. The founder of the company will normally tell you that you can make thousands of pounds a week. What could possibly go wrong?

7. Invest when you're up against a deadline. Every year, thousands of people put their money into the stock market in the run up to the end of the tax year, April the 5th. If you're one of them, you'll probably find you're far too busy trying to get the paperwork done by the deadline to read all that dull small print!

8. Get emotionally involved with your shares. When they go down, refuse to sell them so you don't have to admit a mistake or accept a loss. And when they go up, refuse to sell them because you're determined to squeeze out every last penny of profit.

9. Put your retirement money into spreads, options, futures, and other arcane investments from the very top of the risk/reward ladder. After you lose your investment, throw more money after it by signing up for an expensive seminar by an expert who promises to teach you a secret, can't-miss method for making it all back.

10. Follow the herd. Invest only in companies that have been praised on the TV news and featured on the cover of business magazines. This helps to guarantee that thousands of other people have rushed to buy the shares, forcing up their price and eliminating most of the profit potential.

GUIDELINE: The don'ts of smart investing are just as important as the do's. Remember, sometimes the best investment is the one you *don't* make.

CHAOS THEORY

'Life is what happens to you while you're busy making other plans,' wrote John Lennon. The unexpected is sure to happen, but the way you deal with it can make all the difference between financial well-being and financial wipeout!

THE TROUBLE WITH
OTHER PEOPLE

Friendship is a wonderful thing – one of life's greatest blessings. So is money. But the wise person tries hard *not* to mix the two.

Don't get me wrong. I'm not saying people ought to be stingy towards their friends. Giving thoughtful gifts, sharing meals and special occasions, and even going on holiday together can all be delightful ways to deepen a friendship. But major loans, investment partnerships, and other financial ties can be deadly to a friendship and ought to be avoided.

One reason is that friends usually have different attitudes towards money. During childhood, we learn money lessons by watching the way our parents earn, save, and spend. We also inherit – consciously or unconsciously – many of their attitudes towards money, from anxiety, pride, irritation, and anger to envy, generosity, and meanness. Many people either adopt the same attitude in their own lives, or react by veering towards the opposite extreme. And because the 'fingerprint' of your financial psychology is likely to be dramatically different from that of your friend, there's ample room for misunderstanding, confusion, and hurt feelings when money and friendship mix.

Therefore, if you do lend money to a friend (for example), don't assume they have exactly the same attitude towards loans as you do. Maybe they'll be meticulous about repaying you; maybe they'll forget and have to be reminded, which is a painfully embarrassing thing for both parties. My advice: if you lend or borrow more than a few pounds, write out the terms and exchange signed copies of the note with your friend. This may seem very formal and businesslike, but the clarity it provides will benefit both parties. If you feel a trifle embarrassed to suggest this, blame your bad memory and make a little joke about it.

Are you the financial caretaker in your social circle? Do people turn to you for funds when they are ill or confronted with a sudden emergency? Do you pick up more than your fair share of the bills for shared activities? If so, don't simply let the situation fester. That can only lead to resentment (conscious or unconscious) and perhaps an ultimate, angry confrontation.

Instead, build up your courage and speak out. Begin with a positive statement – for example, 'Our friendship is truly valuable to me. I'd hate any bad feeling to develop between us and spoil it. So I want to point out something that's been bothering me for a while, just so the air can be clear between us.' Chances are that your friend will understand your point of view and be eager to change the behaviour that has made you uncomfortable. If not, maybe the friendship is not as strong as you'd thought.

Another money problem that can blight a friendship is competitiveness and envy. The best way to avoid this problem is to refuse to play the comparison game. Decide what you want in life and make a plan for achieving it (with the help of the advice in this book). Then pay no attention to the possessions, wealth, or success of your friends and neighbours, whether these are greater or less than yours. If you encounter people who treat worldly goods as a measure of personal worth, don't let their attitude infect you. Admire their new car, congratulate them on their house makeover, and remember that people who feel the need to impress others are fundamentally insecure.

Above all, don't get caught up in trying to keep up with the Joneses. If you do, you'll soon find yourself spending irrationally in a crazy downward spiral that can only end in catastrophic debt.

GUIDELINE: A true friend is someone who appreciates your personal qualities – your kindness, humour, intelligence, generosity, and warmth – not your financial status. Keep money matters at a distance from friendship, and both will have a better chance to thrive.

FOR LOVE OR MONEY

When we fall in love, prudent money management is the last thing on our minds. Remember the euphoria of the early months of a romance? It's a time for extravagant gifts, new clothes, special meals out, champagne, flowers, and weekends together. All of which are lovely, memorable – and very expensive.

Among older or more traditional couples, the man pays for the majority of these treats. But in the twenty-first century women in love can find themselves just as shocked as their partners when the credit card bills arrive. Some couples even find themselves in a competitive spending cycle, as if trying to measure their mutual love in hard currency!

So long as the euphoric spending of young romance doesn't go too far, it's relatively harmless. But love leads to commitment. Every year, millions of couples get married or move in together, forging ties that are financial as well as emotional. And, in most cases, they embark on this adventure with almost no planning and little awareness of their financial compatibility – or lack thereof.

Rather than talk about money, most new couples assume that if they are sexually and emotionally compatible, then financial matters will somehow fall into place. This failure to communicate can destroy a relationship. I know a man who found himself picking up all the restaurant and travel bills for his beautiful new girlfriend – partly as a matter of habit, partly out of

'chivalry', partly because of the giddy carelessness that comes with new love. Three months later, Henry was feeling trapped in the pattern he'd set. He secretly confided to me that he wished Lucy would reciprocate somehow, perhaps by offering to cook for him. Of course, Lucy knew or sensed none of this. She assumed Henry liked to be the giver. She may even have thought he'd be offended if she offered to help pay. Today, their relationship is over, a casualty of their unwillingness to talk openly about money.

In today's world, where both partners are likely to be working, what's the fairest way of splitting the bills? If you earn a similar amount, straight down the middle is the fairest method. But if one partner earns substantially more than the other, why not contribute in proportion to your salary? For example, if she earns double what he earns, she might pay two-thirds of the rent on their shared flat, while he picks up the remaining third.

How soon should a loving couple begin to pool their finances, managing income, spending, and investing together? Don't be in a rush to do this. In any case, you should hold off until you've discussed all the questions on pages 146–47 and considered the legal implications on pages 149–52. Remember, relationships can come to an end. And when they do, both parties should be able to walk away with their heads held high and their financial independence intact. It may seem unromantic to think about such matters in the throes of love, but it's realistic, too, and very necessary.

GUIDELINE: Many modern couples have discovered the benefits of speaking frankly about sex – their likes, dislikes, needs, and fantasies. Now be bold enough to break down the last and strongest taboo: talk about money with the one you love.

MEASURE YOUR MONEY COMPATIBILITY

Before you make any serious commitment to the one you love – such as moving in together, having a child, or getting married – devote an evening to sharing your answers to the questions on these pages. In the process, you'll learn a lot about your partner's desires, fears, dreams, and attitudes – and your own as well. If you discover that your deepest values are even more compatible than you'd anticipated, congratulations! You may be a match made in heaven. And if you discover just the opposite, well, be glad you learned the truth today rather than later.

- If you won a million pounds, what would you do with it? (*Some would quit their jobs and devote themselves to high living; others would donate the money to charity; still others would launch the business they'd always imagined. Comparing dreams with your partner is a good way to find out whether your values are compatible.*)
- What is your dream job? How does it compare to what you are doing today? Do you have a plan to achieve your dream job?
- When would you like to retire? What do you see yourself doing in retirement? Do you have a plan to fund this kind of retirement?
- Did your mother and father have different attitudes towards money? Did they ever fight over it? Which parent do you most resemble in this respect? Which relatives did you

admire for their financial skills? Which were useless? (*An in-depth conversation about the ways money was viewed in both your families will cast a great deal of light on your present attitudes.*)

- Do you hope to have children? If so, how many? Would you want to educate them privately? Do you have a plan for managing the expense of child-rearing? (*I'm amazed to find how many couples don't discuss these crucial issues before they dispense with the birth control. Don't assume that your partner knows and shares your expectations about who will support the family during the early years – that simply may not be true.*)
- Do you have any significant savings or investments? If so, which of your investments have been the most lucrative? Which have done poorly? What have you learned from these experiences?
- If you lost your job and had to cut your spending, what would you eliminate?
- Do you go through your bank statements once a month and pay all your bills on time?
- How many credit cards do you have? Do you pay them off every month?
- How often do you visit the cash machine? Do you have a set amount of cash that you take out each time? How do you keep track of your spending? (*If you or your partner are unable to answer these questions, beware! It's going to be very hard for you to keep your joint finances from conflict or even disaster.*)

As you talk, notice the underlying assumptions each of you is making, and think about the dreams, fears, and insecurities you have about money. Be upfront about your values, and pay close attention to your partner's. Above all, don't assume you'll be able to change your loved one's behaviour. If your partner is careless, wasteful, irresponsible, miserly, obsessive, or destructive with money, it'll be very, very difficult for them to change those attitudes and behaviours, no matter how much he or she loves you. In such a case, you need to face the problem with as much realism and honesty as you can muster and decide: can I live with my partner's money personality? Or is it possible that I would be dooming myself to a life of frustration and heartache if I try? It's a painful question – but one that only you can answer.

GUIDELINE: Experience shows that two people do not have to agree about everything in order to live happily together. In most relationships, there are small differences in attitudes about money (and other topics) that may add to the spice of life. But significant differences in fundamental values can be devastating. So don't ignore them.

YOUR VERY OWN LOVE CONTRACT

Whenever you enter a long-term commitment, it makes good sense to be clear about your joint finances. Who owns what? Who is responsible for which expenses? Clarifying issues like these can prevent misunderstandings and squabbles while the relationship is intact and ease the painful process of break-up or divorce (if it happens). Paradoxically, by reducing money tensions, a prenup may actually help couples avoid the need for a split.

Prenups are not legally enforceable in England, Wales or Northern Ireland. In Scotland they may be legally enforceable, although it will depend on a range of factors, such as where the agreement was drawn up. Prenups are least likely to be taken into account once children are involved. Judges are required to consider questions of equity (fairness) and to safeguard the interests of the children when deciding whether and how to respect the terms of the prenup. The guidance of a lawyer can help ensure that your prenup is worded so it conveys your intentions clearly and accurately, although this may not maximize the chances of it being enforced. Still, creating a prenup is a useful exercise because it gives you a plan to work from at a difficult time when your emotions may be all over the place.

When you discuss your 'love contract' with your partner, there are some key issues to cover.

- Who owns the property in which you live? Who owns any other properties that either of you had bought separately? Who pays the mortgage or rent? (Basically, the person whose name is on the title deed is the legal owner. Does this reflect your understanding and intentions?)
- Who owns other valuable property, such as cars, paintings, jewellery, and investments? Do they belong to Partner A, Partner B, or are they joint property of both partners?
- Will you be responsible for any debts run up by your partner? By law, either partner is liable for an overdrawn joint account. And either signatory on a joint account can empty it at will. For this reason, I recommend keeping separate personal accounts as well. If you have two credit cards on the same account, it is the person who signed the agreement who is responsible for the debt, regardless of who uses the card the most.
- Are you responsible for your partner's children from a previous relationship? How should they be cared for in the event of a break-up?
- Would you support your partner if they were made redundant or became too ill to work? (If you live together, the Department for Work and Pensions will take your joint income and savings into account when deciding whether either partner is entitled to state benefits.)

If you want further information or an example of a 'living together agreement', I'd suggest you visit the website of the independent legal advice service: www.advicenow.org.uk.

Your contract should incorporate your wills, which outline what should happen to your belongings when you die, either separately or together (see pages 208–13).

Having a will is particularly important if one of the families disapproves of your relationship. Without a will, a surviving unmarried partner who is estranged from the in-laws may end up destitute as well as bereaved. A spouse does have some legal rights and will inherit something. In either case, a will makes your intent clear and the situation neater.

Discuss all these matters with your partner until you reach an agreement you're both happy with. Don't rush through the process! It will probably take a few sessions to think through all the implications of these decisions and come to a consensus that is fair to both partners. Then ask a lawyer to put the crucial points into writing in a legal document.

GUIDELINE: If you're worried that your partner may recoil at the notion of a prenuptial agreement, hand them this book – with a bookmark inserted at this page. By reducing financial uncertainty and enhancing mutual trust, a prenup should strengthen, not damage, your love.

THE TRUE COST OF YOUR BIG DAY

People who are normally quite sane with their money can find themselves getting a touch of Posh & Becks syndrome as their wedding day approaches. (I've even met couples who tried to emulate that famous wedding, right down to the crowns and thrones.) Lavish reporting about celebrity weddings has done a lot to contribute to the UK's record-breaking levels of consumer debt. Many read *Hello!* and *OK!* and conclude, 'I'm just as deserving as Victoria Beckham.' Maybe so, but she has millions of pounds in the bank, and you don't – at least not yet.

Given the massive emotional, social, and cultural implications of marriage, it's not surprising that money tensions often surface during the process of planning a wedding. Should the bride's family pay for everything, or should costs be split down the middle? What if it's a second or third marriage? What if one family is well-to-do, while the other is struggling? I've heard horror stories about weddings that have gone wrong over money strife, including one where the groom's family started a punch-up because the bride's father had arranged to switch to a pay bar at a certain point in the evening.

Modern brides and grooms often pay for their own weddings, both to avoid family arguments and to retain control over the details. The average cost of the ceremony and reception is currently around £20,000, and managing this budget is often the first big challenge of the couple's new life together. How will they raise the money? Who will handle the dozens of decisions to be made? Will bride and groom be able to reach amicable compromises when the inevitable disagreements arise?

My advice is to start by setting the total amount you want to spend. Then stick to your budget, even if this requires an occasional sacrifice. What if the bride falls in love with a dress that costs £100 more than you'd budgeted? Consider supplying fewer bottles of champagne, or cut a couple of guests from the sit-down dinner. Should you invite his Auntie Maud and Uncle Harold, even if it means dropping that old school friend who invited you to her wedding last year? Work these kinds of issues through

together, and you'll be learning important lessons about the give and take of married life.

Above all, make a conscious effort to keep your sense of humour. You'll both feel under enormous pressure from parents, friends, wedding 'consultants', and 'advisers', and even from images in the media, to make your wedding into a 'perfect' reflection of your unique love. This dream of perfection easily morphs into an unreasonable obsession with details that are ultimately trivial – as though your marriage will be blighted if you can't have orchids of just the perfect shade of violet.

Remember that this is not why you fell in love in the first place. And ask any old married couple – they'll agree that the most vivid and enjoyable memories from their wedding are the moments they didn't plan, when 'perfection' was forgotten and joyous spontaneity took over.

GUIDELINE: A wedding can put enormous stress on the most solid relationship. Don't let this happen to you. Maintain your perspective, avoid getting carried away by the impulse to overspend, and make the planning process an opportunity to practise the virtues of married life: mutual acceptance, good humour, and forgiveness.

CONFLICT RESOLUTION

According to the relationship counselling service Relate, money is one of the biggest causes of arguments among couples. Research by the Financial Services Authority (FSA) showed that 75 per cent of couples found money the hardest subject to talk about. Sex, children, in-laws, and whose turn it is to take out the rubbish came further down the list. And money arguments can be among the hardest to resolve because our self-esteem is so tied up with money and how we spend it that any criticism can feel like a deeply personal attack.

If you've discussed your money attitudes and agreed to a plan in the event of a break-up, then at least the ground rules should be clear. But marriage or any other long-term commitment is all about coping with change. A comfortable balance may be upset if one partner starts earning significantly more than the other when you used to be more or less equal. Loss of a job, pregnancy and parenthood, illness or disability, and inheritance are other life-changing events that can produce financial disagreements and discord.

If you and your partner find yourselves arguing about money, try this simple method of conflict resolution. Start by listing everything you would like to change about your partner's money habits. Be specific and use non-emotional, non-judgmental language. Rather than writing, 'I wish he would be more responsible,' write, 'I wish he would take over paying the bills each month.' Rather than, 'I wish she wouldn't waste money,' write, 'I wish she would consult me before spending more than £100 from our joint account.'

Then swap lists and discuss what you've written. You may well discover that most of the nagging irritants in your relationship can be fixed fairly easily, just by changing a handful of behaviours.

If there are areas of intense disagreement, talk them through. Discuss the *feelings* that underlie the behaviour. Perhaps you (or your partner) spend money impulsively to alleviate the resentment you feel over being trapped in a job you dislike. Perhaps you become unreasonably angry when your partner splurges on a treat because to you this short-term pleasure feels like he or she is stealing or squandering money that would help to achieve a long-term goal that you have not made clear to your partner.

Sometimes simply recognizing and discussing the emotions attached to money can go a long way towards reducing the stress and anger in a relationship. The conversation may also point the way towards a change in behaviour that may help solve the problem. Perhaps you should take an evening class to prepare yourself for a new career you'll find more rewarding; perhaps you should make an effort to learn to spend money on your own enjoyment (in moderation, of course). And when disagreements persist, look for ways to compromise: have one partner accept the other's minor eccentricity in exchange for a similar indulgence going the opposite way.

Tackle the easiest changes first. After a couple of weeks, add the next easiest. Keep discussing your progress and watch out for back-sliding, but don't lower yourself to petty score-keeping. Honour the spirit of your agreement and keep your sense of humour. Don't be like the husband of a friend of mine who wakened her one morning to ask why she had opened a new bar of soap for the sink when there was one already open in the shower. She replied: 'Darling, pretend for a minute that there's someone else in the room and try to imagine how you would look through their eyes.' Not a bad retort.

If you and your partner find it impossible to create and carry out a plan for sharing your finances without hostility, perhaps the relationship ought to be reconsidered. It's dangerous to assume that you can change a person *fundamentally*. If you have a partner who is extremely irresponsible or selfish and who is unwilling or unable to change, don't allow them to destroy your financial future. Save yourself, even if it means a painful break-up. Being a victim benefits no one in the long run.

GUIDELINE: It's hard work to keep the lines of communication about money open. But it's the only way to ensure that both partners feel, deep down, that their shared financial arrangements are fair, thereby avoiding the hidden resentment that in time can undermine and destroy a relationship.

DEALING WITH A DEBT-AHOLIC

An addiction is terrible. It can ruin your health, destroy your relationships, and blight your life. And though addictions to substances like alcohol, cocaine, and heroin are among the best known, one of today's fastest growing and most destructive addictions is spending.

The average person in the UK owes nearly £4,850 (excluding mortgage debt). Since a sizeable percentage of the population has no debt at all, that means there are many who owe much more than this.

Earlier in this book, I showed you how to manage your own debt problem. But if you have a partner who is a compulsive debt-aholic, you have a different problem that can be even more difficult to solve. It doesn't matter whether the spending is for clothes, holidays, home improvements, or just living beyond their means all round; if your partner is running up unmanageable debt, your first priority should be to make sure you don't get dragged down, too.

The organization Alcoholics Anonymous (AA) has long dealt with this phenomenon in relation to excessive drinking, and their advice applies to overspending as well. One of the first steps in helping an addict to overcome addiction is to withdraw outside support for the bad habit. In the case of a spending addict, you must stop paying their debts. Separate your finances and open a bank account in your name only so that the debt-aholic doesn't have access to money that you earn or that is earmarked for household bills. Revise your partnership agreement and make sure that your partner's creditors won't be able to bankrupt you should the worst come to the worst.

There's an association for compulsive spenders called Debtors' Anonymous, which uses techniques similar to AA (see page 242 for contact details). More than half your problem will probably lie in convincing your partner that he or she really *is* a debt-aholic, because most debt addicts are in deep denial. They have many excuses: 'Everyone else carries debt – why shouldn't I?', or 'Something always happens to keep me from catching up with my debts.' Don't let the debt-aholic use these excuses to buy a reprieve. They will only take the opportunity to sink deeper into a miasma of unmanageable debt.

Above all, remember that you are under no moral obligation to allow an out-of-control partner to destroy your life along with their own. If you are partnered with a debt-aholic who refuses to take the necessary steps to get the spending under control, you may have no choice but to end the relationship – for the sake of your own survival.

GUIDELINE: Use tough love if your partner is spending compulsively. Take control of your shared finances and cut off the flow of credit that feeds the debt-aholic's addiction. Make sure it's only their money they can squander, not yours. And beware of the emotional blackmail inherent in lines like, 'If you really loved me, you would help me out of this mess.'

SAVING FOR BABY

Becoming a parent is one of the most dramatic life changes you can experience. In addition to a new world of joys, anxieties, surprises, fears, and satisfactions, parenthood will reshape your financial life. Your income will probably go down, at least temporarily, while your expenses will go up. Planning for the money adjustments you'll have to make is even more important than buying a pram or painting a bedroom that special baby colour.

Let's start with the effects on your income. Nearly every mother takes significant time off during and after the birth of her baby. Statutory maternity pay is currently set at 90 per cent of your average gross weekly earnings for the first six weeks, followed by £123.06 for the next 33 weeks or 90 per cent of your average earnings if it is less than £123.06. To qualify for statutory maternity pay, you have to earn a minimum average gross wage of £95 a week. Paternity pay is set at £123.06 or 90 per cent of your average weekly earnings, if this is less, for one or two weeks. Any additional time off you may take will probably be unpaid, but check with your employer. Men are entitled to two weeks' paternity leave on full pay.

If either parent thinks he or she will want to take more than the statutory paid leave, I strongly suggest building a savings cushion to tide you over. Otherwise, you'll be starting baby's life accumulating a mountain of debt, which will add relationship stress later on.

After baby is born, some women find they can't bear to go back to work even if they had previously planned to. Other

mothers find that the costs of childcare eat up most of their salary, negating the financial benefits of having a job. And of course, some new mothers or babies encounter unexpected health concerns that prevent mum from working. For these reasons, I advise couples who plan to have children to budget as if they will have to live on only one income – since, in many cases, this turns out to be true.

Unfortunately, mothers can also expect to find their long-term earning potential somewhat diminished by the time they take for parenthood. Studies show that the average woman who has children in her early twenties and stops work until they start school will cut her lifetime salary by about *half*.

On the other hand, if you have babies in your late twenties or early thirties and take only the statutory twelve months maternity leave, you can reduce the impact on your earnings considerably.

This *doesn't* mean that it's a mistake to have children young and take time off from work to raise them. I just want you to plan carefully so you can enjoy parenthood to the fullest.

Then there's the expense side of the equation. Current estimates are that it costs some £194,000 to raise a child to the age of eighteen (and much more than this if you opt for private education). Fortunately, you don't have to find all this money upfront before starting a family. The early years are relatively less demanding. Nappies and squishy foods are fairly cheap. However the costs will gradually increase over the years as the children progress from Lego to PlayStations. Hopefully your career will improve in parallel, so that you'll be able to afford the expenses as they arise.

GUIDELINE: When you're planning a family, create a new budget that reflects the many changes you expect. Do not underestimate the financial pressures of parenthood. Learning to care for a new life is challenging enough without worrying about money too.

EDUCATING RITA (OR RICKY)

In today's competitive world, a good education is more important than ever. Financial planning for parenthood is incomplete unless you take into account the costs of providing your kids with the kind of schooling they will need to keep up with their peers – not just in Britain, but around the world.

Parents living in the UK tell me that getting into decent state schools can be like a postcode lottery. You move into the catchment area for a top-flight school, then find they've shifted the boundary. Feeling frustrated and anxious, many parents are opting for private education. It's a costly alternative. The average private school fee is around £9,000 per year per child, and you can treble that if they're boarding. Expect the cost to rise by around 5 per cent a year, giving a total bill of over £150,000 per child. Can you afford to pay this amount for two children, or three?

Before you opt for private schooling, be sure it's really necessary. My experience and observation suggest that the important thing is to instil in your child a love of reading, a curiosity about the world around them, and the tools to discover knowledge for themselves. If you do this, your child will probably grow into a smart, knowledgeable, and skilled adult no matter which school he or she attends.

If you choose to go private, start putting money aside as soon as possible. You can use tax-free investment plans, such as ISAs and tax-free accounts offered by National

Savings and Investments (see page 245). Start your plan with the £250 the government is offering for every child born after 1 September 2002 through the Child Trust Fund. Ask grandparents or other relatives to contribute as well. It's a far better focus for family generosity than the mountains of clothes and toys many children receive at Christmas and for birthdays.

I've been listening with interest to the debate in the UK over who should pay for university education. More and more students will clearly have to do what I did: I paid for part of my college expenses by taking jobs that fitted around the hours when I had classes and during my summer vacation. I also took out loans and had to pay them off after I graduated. I did not resent this either

during college or after I graduated. I know the burden of the loans made me defer some of the things I wanted to do. At the time, my impatience made me keenly aware of the sacrifice and frustration. But I always reminded myself that the true benefits of a good education are long term.

I think it is character-building for students to contribute towards their own living expenses while studying for a degree. Importantly, it can also give a young person a realistic sense of how to manage money, an essential skill for the many people who leave university with large amounts of debt. It can help make the university years into a good transition to the adult world where we have to look after ourselves – and set financial priorities.

Don't be afraid of student loans. They are a very cheap way to borrow money. Interest is charged in line with inflation, and you don't have to start making repayments until you are earning a salary of more than £15,000 a year, at which point you pay 9 per cent of the amount you earn over that. So, if you had a salary of £20,000, you would repay £450 per year (£5,000 x 9% = £450). This is only £37.50 a month. Not bad for a good education!

GUIDELINE: A university education is a worthwhile investment, even if you must work part-time to pay for it. Remember that over the long term, you are likely to have a higher future earning power and a more interesting career than those who didn't get a degree. This means your schooling will pay off in both financial and non-financial ways for the rest of your life.

RESISTING PESTER POWER

Of all the personal values we pass along to our children, perhaps none is as powerful as consumerism. Watch half an hour of kids' TV and you can see why. The commercial breaks are full of racing cars, cuddly toys, dolls with all kinds of special talents, and an array of merchandise tied to the latest hit movies. The stream is endless, and it gets worse in the run-up to Christmas.

Television isn't the only place where our children are taught the importance of spending. Supermarkets devote entire aisles to toys, newsagents sell comics with plastic gifts attached, and even an educational outing to a museum or safari park includes a detour to the gift shop. As a

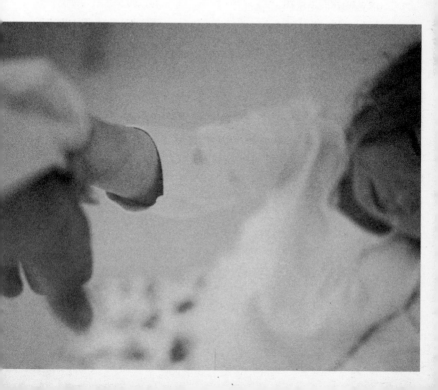

result, even the youngest children are often enthusiastic participants in consumer culture.

What can a parent do about the constant tugging at your sleeve and the urgent cries of, 'I *want* that'?

Some just cave in. The motives are varied. Some parents feel guilty if their children don't have as many toys as their playmates. Others buy presents to compensate for the fact they can't spend as much quality time with their kids as they would like. Some harassed parents give in to their child's whining in an effort to win a moment's peace – a very short-term solution, since you've just taught the child that whining works!

If any of these scenarios sounds familiar, get a grip on yourself! A parent's role is not to give their children everything they want at the moment they want it. What kind of unrealistic lesson would that be teaching them about life and the world?

The best gift you can give to your children is the ability to solve problems and cope with whatever life throws at them – with or without the help of material possessions. Set boundaries on gift-giving. When buying a treat is appropriate, offer your child a limited choice: 'You can't have both X and Y, but you can choose one of them.' After they've chosen, make them live with their decision. Don't go back and buy the second gift later. In this way, you will help your child learn to control their appetites and think about long-term happiness rather than immediate gratification.

From an early age, your child should be taught that there are 'big' presents that are appropriate only at Christmas or for a birthday. Children can develop a rough idea of what money is from around the age of three. You can explain that toys cost money, and that money is not an unlimited commodity but that you have to work to earn it. More complicated money lessons – such as the importance of saving and sharing, as well as the value of money, can wait until they are older.

Above all, straighten out your own thinking about money. If you tend to overspend as a way of coping with frustration, loneliness, or disappointment, your children will probably learn to do the same. If you manage money with maturity and self-discipline, your kids are more likely to do so.

GUIDELINE: In relating to your children, don't use money, gifts, toys, or treats as a symbol or substitute for love. Instead, help your children learn that their self-esteem shouldn't be dependent on material possessions – that their hearts and minds are what make them truly precious.

CREATING THE TYCOONS OF TOMORROW

Parents sometimes ask me what they can do to teach their children about wise money management. My best advice is to remember the golden rule of parenting: that children will usually do what they see you doing rather than what you *tell* them to do. If you want them to learn to be good at managing money, let them see you acting responsibly. Avoid buying on impulse, letting bills accumulate, and going into debt. Instead, let your children see you thinking about major purchases and saving for your future (and theirs).

I'm a firm believer in giving children pocket money and letting them learn how to manage it. Start your children on an allowance around the age of five. Encourage them to save up for a few weeks to afford treats they want rather than squandering their money on sweets straight away. Make it clear that they can't come back for more if they blow it all quickly. And make sure that grandparents, uncles and aunts back you up on this.

One grown woman told me that she can still remember the shock of the day when, at the age of eight, she lost a pound from her purse. In tears, she told her mother, expecting that it would be replaced. After all, wasn't Mummy the person who made everything right in the world? Instead, her mother said, 'Oh dear. That will teach you to be more careful next time.' And indeed it did.

Tie the allowance to your child's age, increasing the sum a little on each birthday. If you like, you can offer extra cash if your child does some chores round the house. I don't mean everyday family tasks like setting the table or tidying their room (which they should be doing anyway), but bigger jobs such as washing the car or weeding the flowerbed. Agree on the going rate for a range of tasks and then see how much they want the money!

Around the age of eight, begin teaching your child to save. Many banks and building societies offer children's savings accounts with a range of incentives such as free piggy banks, stickers, club membership, magazines, and the chance to compete for valuable prizes such as family trips to EuroDisney or a home computer. If you help your child to catch the savings habit young, then maybe they won't have to read books like this when they're older!

Many leaders of industry – the Richard Bransons and Bill Gateses of the world – started their first businesses while they were still at school. I'm not saying you should push your children to do the same, but it's important for a child to know the value of money and understand the link between hard work and achievement. Kids who grow up that way enjoy greater self-esteem and are better prepared to accomplish great things when they are out in the world.

GUIDELINE: Don't be shy about teaching your children the financial facts of life. Letting them remain ignorant about money won't preserve their innocence; it will simply leave them ill-equipped to deal with an increasingly challenging world.

THE BOOMERANG GENERATION

The traditional assumption about raising children is that once they finish school they should be ready to face the world alone. But for some young people today, the world is an overwhelming place. In reaction, they flee to the only source of help and comfort they've known: Mum and Dad. Their car's broken down and they can't afford to fix it, so they leave it in your driveway. They don't have a washing machine, so they drop off their bags of dirty laundry. Or they spend all their money at the beginning of the month and come to you for a handout. These are the kids I call the Boomerang Generation.

Of course, it's not supposed to be this way. But when it happens, the lion's share of blame usually belongs with the parents. If your children can't cope with the outside world, maybe it's because you didn't give them the tools to cope. Maybe you've been making decisions for them instead of encouraging them to come up with their own solutions to problems. I call this 'managing' rather than 'nurturing', and it only slows the growing-up process.

Some parents behave this way for emotional or psychological reasons. Some who aren't ready to let go of their 'babies' set up a dynamic (consciously or not) that encourages the child to keep coming back. I hear some parents describe a child as 'my best friend'. No, they're not; they're your offspring. Other parents like to cluck over their child's inadequacies: 'He never feeds himself properly,' they'll say, or, 'She's useless at remembering to buy lightbulbs.' They don't realize that they are

infantilizing their grown-up children when they turn up with a sackful of groceries and 'a little extra' to tide them over.

By the time a person is eighteen years old, he or she is an adult and should be treated as such. My mother always made it very clear to her children that we would have to be ready to support ourselves when we were eighteen. It made me think long and hard about what I was going to do and how I was going to manage, so when the time came I was ready for it.

If you are the parents of a boomerang child (or children), then it's time to cut the apron strings. Stop bailing them out. If they desperately need money and you are able and willing to help, make them a loan in businesslike fashion. Write out a letter of agreement stating the repayments they have to make and the interest you will charge. If they default on repayments, they don't get any more loans. That's the deal.

And if you are a boomerang child yourself, just grow up! Learn to stand on your own two feet.

GUIDELINE: When you're teaching your kids to ride a bike, you have to take the stabilizers off at some point and let them go off on their own. It's the same thing when they leave home.

OVERCOMING WARDROBE MANIA

Clothes are one of the most common obsessions among chronic overspenders. There are various psychological reasons for this form of financial self-abuse. For some people, an expensive wardrobe is a symbol of status or success; for others, a way of expressing their individuality; for still others, a gesture of defiance against an otherwise drab existence. The one thing that many people who overspend on clothes tend to have in common is low self-esteem. They are trying to influence the way the world perceives them by the clothes they wear, rather than relying on their inner qualities to win respect and affection.

To overcome an addiction to clothes shopping, you'll need to set strict limits on yourself. Unlike alcohol, tobacco, or heroin, which an addict can (and should) give up completely, you can't go 'cold turkey' on clothes shopping, because people aren't allowed to wander around naked. The following rules will help you keep your habit under control on those occasions when you really *need* to buy something to wear.

- At the beginning of each season, look through your wardrobe to see what you need, then walk around your favourite shops *without* your credit cards, just to see what's available.
- Before making any clothes purchase, observe a cooling-off period of 48 hours. Ask the shop to put the garment aside, reconsider your annual clothing budget, and think about

what you are about to buy for two days. Quite often you'll find that your enthusiasm has faded before the time comes to make the purchase.

- When money is tight, avoid temptation. Don't go near your favourite shops and avoid well-to-do friends whose clothes make you feel insecure or envious. And don't go shopping as recreation or a means of coping with the blues.

- Don't let a sale lure you into buying something you don't need. When you buy a £200 coat for £150, you're not saving £50 – you're *spending* £150!

- When it comes to fashion, think timeless, not timely. The very latest looks are the ones most likely to seem dated six months down the road. What's the point in spending a fortune on something you'll only wear for a season?

- Buy clothes with multiple purposes, in styles and colours that mix and match easily with other garments you own. The more versatile the clothes you buy, the more use you'll get out of them.

- Try leaving your credit card at home and force yourself to pay cash for new clothes. Peeling off fivers from your wallet is a great way to focus your mind on whether you're paying for something you really need.

GUIDELINE: Set an annual spending budget for clothes and stick to it. And remember – if you blow the lot on summer clothes, you're going to get a bit chilly in the autumn!

TECHNO SHOPPING

Electrical and electronic gadgets are a necessity of modern life. All homeowners need 'white goods' (fridges, cookers, washing machines) for their kitchens, most of us have entertainment systems, and almost half of all households now have a home computer. Unfortunately, few people are experts on how to choose and purchase high-tech gear. That's why I recommend devoting some time to research and study before you buy. It's also worth spending some time doing a little research into the company you're buying from. The last thing you want is to buy from a retailer that won't be around long enough to make the delivery.

For most of us, the web is a really useful source of information, but if anything, there seem to be too many websites that aim to take the strain out of shopping around. So here are a few of my favourites to get you started. www.pricerunner.co.uk is worth checking out, as are www.kelkoo.co.uk and www.ciao.co.uk. I've listed more sites on page 247. I'd definitely advise you to look up consumer reviews of products before you take the plunge. Just type the make and model of the goods you're looking to buy and the word 'problem' or 'complaint' into Google and it's normally enough to do the trick! You can also pick up scratched or slightly damaged appliances from auction sites of the major electrical retailers. Only use these sites if you're not the kind of person who gets carried away in the heat of the moment.

If you don't have access to a computer at home or at work, try visiting an internet café to do your on-line research. You can also try consumer magazines such as *Which?* and *Good Housekeeping*. Both carry out research and test products. You can subscribe and have *Which?* magazine delivered monthly, or you can get information direct from their website (www.whichmagazine.co.uk).

When buying a high-tech item like a computer, digital camera, or DVD player, one way to save is by buying last year's model. Prices usually plummet on equipment that the aficionado considers outdated, although the specifications are usually fine for the average user.

When you visit an electrical goods shop, it's always worth trying to negotiate on price with the sales staff, especially if you are buying more than one item. If they refuse to drop the price, ask if they can throw in free delivery or an additional accessory. There's so much

competition out there, you could well talk your way into a better deal.

Beware of salespeople trying to persuade you to take out extended warranties. Research shows that paying for any needed repairs yourself will almost certainly cost you less. Some level of manufacturer's warranty should be included in the purchase price, with one year's free warranty as a basic minimum. If you buy from supermarkets or department stores, they may have their own warranty schemes in place, and some offer three or four years' cover without an additional fee. And if you accidentally damage your goods, they may be covered under your household contents insurance (only if you have chosen accidental damage cover).

GUIDELINE: Always do your research on high-tech purchases, and bargain over price. Do some research into the company you're buying from and pay with a credit card if you can. If the product doesn't arrive or the company goes bust, you'll be able to make a claim on your credit card (as long as the goods cost over £100 and less than £30,000).

CONNOISSEURS' CORNER

Do you enjoy buying art, ceramics, jewellery, or fine wines for your cellar? Do you have a unique collection of art deco lamps, Victorian dolls, or Clarice Cliff pottery? A hobby like this can be a wonderful source of lifelong entertainment and satisfaction. I know – I collect art, especially photography and drawings.

However, it's a mistake to assume that collectibles can be a cornerstone of your investment strategy. Remember the distinction between liquid and illiquid assets? Art, antiques, and other collectibles definitely fall into the illiquid category. If you need to sell your collection quickly because of a pressing financial need, it may take a while to find a buyer and it's unlikely you will be able to realize the full value.

Collectibles have other drawbacks as an investment. The future value of your collection is almost impossible to predict, because it will be based on popular preferences and tastes, which are notoriously fickle. And unlike a savings account or an investment in shares, bonds, or unit trusts, a collection doesn't produce a steady stream of dividend or interest income while you own it.

If you are spending serious money on art or other collectibles, always consult a specialist adviser. If you go to auctions, take a friend who knows your upper price limit and will remind you about it if bidding fever strikes. Experts say it's best to choose a small area and collect in depth: nineteenth-century French paperweights, rather than any paperweights that catch your eye; Rupert Bear memorabilia rather than any old teddy bears; Chinese snuff bottles rather than all the pretty glassware you come across.

If you like modern art and have high hopes of discovering the next young genius, go to galleries that have a reputation for discovering new artists and nurturing their careers. And don't expect all of them to become the next artist with a waiting list of collectors. I made a few mistakes back in the 1980s when I bought some large paintings from 'up-and-coming' artists who've never been heard of since. I have an antique chair that's worth less than a third of what I paid for it. I've also made some great finds that have risen substantially in value. Overall, I'm way ahead in terms of profit.

When you buy valuable items, think carefully about where you will store them and what the insurance costs will be. Make sure you know the proper procedures for preserving, restoring, and protecting items such as old furniture, fabrics, paintings, and books. Well-meaning but uninformed collectors have sometimes caused thousands of pounds' worth of damage by cleaning their prize purchases incorrectly.

GUIDELINE: Collecting objects can be a wonderful hobby, but don't expect your collection to finance your retirement or the kids' education. Instead, collect things you love and will enjoy having around, even if they don't increase in value.

BUYING ON-LINE

The popularity of broadband – rather than the internet itself – has encouraged more of us to shop on-line. And why wouldn't you? It's a great way of avoiding the weekend rush. You can track down obscure items that you would struggle to find elsewhere – in a matter of minutes.

And then there are the savings. You won't always get something cheaper on-line than you'd be able to buy on the high street, but you can easily compare prices to make sure you're getting a good deal.

The on-line auction house eBay is still hugely popular for everything from collectibles to jewellery, gadgets, toys – even cars and caravans. Unfortunately, it's also where some unscrupulous traders sell fakes.

While many of us are happy to shop on-line, research carried out by the Office of Fair Trading showed that a third of shoppers were too worried about fraud to hand over their credit card details. However, there are steps you can take to reduce the risks of fraudulent transactions.

- Download and use up-to-date antivirus software, download security patches as they're released and make sure your firewall is switched on. If you don't do this, your PC could be infected by a virus or spyware, which means criminals could get access to your bank or card details and passwords.
- Look out for marks that show the site is secure such as a golden padlock symbol (but only if this appears on the bottom of the screen or the browser bar, not within the page of the screen itself) or for web addresses beginning https:// (the 's' stands for 'secure'). Alternatively, look for shops that have signed up to safebuy.org.uk.

- Get the supplier's postal address and telephone number before you give your details, and keep a note of what you have ordered plus the supplier's confirmation notice.
- Read the supplier's terms and conditions, including their returns policy. When dealing with a company, you have the same legal right to return faulty goods as you would if you bought them in a traditional retail store (see pages 186–7). You can take them out of the wrapper (unless they're goods such as CDs or DVDs where you could use them), but you normally have to pay the return postage. The same may not be true if you buy from a private vendor at an internet auction site.
- If your credit or debit card is used fraudulently, the bank or card company should refund the money that has been stolen, unless you've not acted with reasonable care. If they refuse, you can take your complaint to the Financial Ombudsman Service (see page 249 for details). I'd also recommend paying by credit card if the goods cost more than £100 and less than £30,000, because then you can get your money back from the credit card company if the goods don't arrive or the company goes bust.

Even if you plan to make your purchase at a regular retail shop, consider researching price and product specifications on-line. If you spend a few minutes comparing bargains from a dozen internet retailers, you may be able to come up with a low-end price that a neighbourhood store will match.

GUIDELINE: Internet shopping is usually safe and secure, provided you have taken steps to protect your PC and you use a reputable on-line retailer. See page 242 for organizations that can help if you have a problem with on-line shopping.

DON'T GET RIPPED OFF

Over the past generation, consumers in the UK and around the world have become steadily better informed and more aggressive about asserting their rights. This is an excellent trend. The majority of businesses are run by honest, reliable people who want to give you your money's worth. So when a product you buy proves to be defective or unsuitable, most companies will work with you to solve the problem fairly.

Here are some tips that will help you achieve satisfaction when a consumer dispute arises.

- In the UK, the Sale of Goods Act states that goods sold to you must be of satisfactory quality, and fit for the purpose specified by the buyer. These rights last for up to six years, although it doesn't mean that *all* goods have to last this long. The goods should also conform to the way they are described on any packaging or advertising. If not, you are entitled to a refund. If the retailer refuses, report them to your local Trading Standards Department.

- If you find that an item you've bought is defective or damaged, return it to the shop you bought it from. If the problem occurs within the first six months, it's down to the retailer to show the goods were not defective, not the other way round. Even if the fault develops after six months, you may be entitled to a repair or replacement, or a full or partial refund if it can't be repaired or replaced. Don't be fobbed off by the store trying to get you to make a claim under the manufacturer's warranty. Your contract is with the retailer, not the manufacturer. EU law specifies you can ask for a replacement for up to two years after you bought the goods, even if the guarantee only lasts for 12 months.

- However, you are not entitled to a refund if a) you caused the damage yourself, b) you want to change something because you have seen it cheaper elsewhere, c) you accidentally bought the wrong size, d) you bought the goods more than six years ago, e) you were told of the fault before you bought the item or it would have been reasonable to notice it on examination.

- If you want to return an item that is not defective or damaged, you don't have any legal right to change it. However many high-street shops will allow you to exchange it or give you a credit note, as long as the item doesn't show signs of wear or tear. Their terms regarding returns should be clearly stated in writing on a notice near the till in the shop.

- You don't need to provide a till receipt, but try to give some proof of purchase, such as a credit card statement. If the item cost more than £100 and you bought it on a credit card, the card company has joint liability.

- Your rights still apply if you bought the goods in a sale, unless they were described as faulty at the time. During sale time, some shops display signs saying that normal consumer rights don't apply. This is illegal.

GUIDELINE: Return the goods as soon as you spot a fault. Although the Sale of Goods Act gives you valuable protection that lasts for up to six years, the earlier you complain the easier it is to get a repair, replacement or refund. Don't accept store credit unless you have no other choice. They're often a good deal for the shop because lots of people forget to use them.

HAPPY HOLIDAYS

Thirty years ago, it was common practice to leaf through travel brochures in January and decide where you wanted to spend your two weeks' holiday in the summer. You then put down a deposit and made monthly payments so that the trip was paid for before you set foot on the plane or in the hotel.

Some people still do this, but the common practice in the twenty-first century is to book last-minute holidays on high-interest credit cards. This means that you haven't actually forked out a penny while you're lazing on a sun lounger or touring the Louvre, but you face a looming cloud of debt on your return.

The holidays themselves have become more costly than ever. Many people feel as though each and every holiday they take must be the 'holiday of a lifetime' (even though we now take more breaks than ever before, with three a year not unusual). They splurge on expensive meals, over-priced swimwear, tropical dance shows, boat trips round the bay, umpteen gifts for the kids, and tacky souvenirs for all their friends — all charged with little thought or restraint on credit cards. The fun is delightful while it lasts, but you'll have to face the music even before the last grains of sand have been shaken out of your trainers.

But holidays needn't send your financial plans into freefall if you allow for them in your monthly budget. Suppose you want three holidays a year. For the sake of argument, let's allocate £3,000 to pay for them. If you put £250 in a savings account every month, the money will be there, waiting, when you next get itchy feet. And what if you can't afford to save that much every month? You know what that means: scale back your travel plans accordingly.

Do research in books or on the internet before you put money down for a package holiday. You might get a better deal buying a low-cost flight and booking your own hotel. Maybe you don't need a luxury hotel if you're not going to be spending much time there – clean, comfortable, and well located might be enough. But remember that if you travel independently, you may not find it so easy to get your money back or to rebook if events mean you have to change your plans. When swine flu (and a few years earlier, the SARS virus) struck, some people had to try and negotiate with airlines and hotels directly – sometimes without success.

If you bought flights directly from the airline, you also won't be covered if it goes bankrupt unless you pay by credit card and the flight(s) costs more than £100. Alternatively, you can buy separate 'airline failure insurance' for just a few pounds. However, you are covered by Air Travel Organisers' Licensing (ATOL) rules if you book a flight via an ATOL-protected tour operator.

For package holidays, make sure the travel agent is a member of The Association of British Travel Agencies (ABTA) which will protect your money or rescue you if your travel agency goes bankrupt and leaves you stranded.

GUIDELINE: Be aware of your rights when booking your holiday. Research the different options and how much protection you would get if things go wrong. Pay by credit card if you can and stick to a budget.

DON'T GET CAUGHT OUT

If you're planning an overseas holiday, you should spend some time working out how you're going to pay for extras (such as meals, trips, and souvenirs) when you're there. Paying by credit card is convenient, but it could be the most expensive option.

And if you're the kind of person who normally buys their holiday money at the airport, you might pay a lot more than you need to.

Here are some tips that will help you get the most from your spending while you're on holiday:

- Compare different currency deals before you buy your holiday money. You will often get the cheapest deal if you buy on-line, although some on-line bureaux de change include a delivery charge if you change less than a minimum amount (which may be several hundred pounds).
- Check to see whether you have to pay extra charges or if everything is included. The easiest way to compare costs is to ask how much you would have to pay to buy €500/$500 or whatever you want to take with you.
- Don't use your credit card to withdraw cash. You will be charged interest from day one at a higher rate than the one you pay on purchases. At time of writing some cards were charging well over 20% for cash withdrawals.
- Debit and credit cards also apply charges for cash withdrawals abroad. Typically you will be charged a cash conversion charge (which could work out at 2.75%) and a cash withdrawal charge (of at least 1.5%).

- If you think you might find it hard to stick to a budget while you're abroad, consider taking a pre-pay currency card that you can load up before you leave. It also means you will not have to carry large amounts of cash around with you.
- Watch out for criminals and fraudsters when you are on holiday. Don't let your credit or debit card out of your sight. Figures from the banking industry show that card fraud is on the rise overseas, particularly in countries that do not have a chip and pin system. (The United States is a favourite location for card fraud.)
- Banks and credit card companies monitor spending patterns and look for transactions that are out of the ordinary. So, before you travel, contact your bank and tell them how long you will be away for and where you plan to go. Your card might still get blocked while you're away, but notifying the bank or company in advance should reduce the chances of it happening. Make sure the bank has an up-to-date mobile number for you, so they can ring you if they suspect fraud has been committed.
- Consider taking a credit and debit card from different banks or providers so that if one card is blocked you will have an alternative.

GUIDELINE: Spend some time working out how to get the most from the money you've set aside for your holiday spending. Use the internet to track down a good deal before you go, and never change money in hotels or street kiosks.

THE UNFORESEEABLES

Bad stuff happens – often when you least expect it. If you've followed all the advice in this book, you'll have at least four months' savings in a liquid account and have bought adequate insurance cover. This will help to cushion you when financial disaster strikes. Otherwise, events like the ones I describe here could push you into catastrophic debt that will be hard to recover from.

In some emergencies, you have to act fast. That's why it's a good idea to think ahead and have a rough game plan in place. In the next few pages, I'll give you the strategies you should use in seven common emergencies, although I sincerely hope none of them will ever happen to you.

Redundancy

When the company you work for is in trouble, there are generally some warning signs: orders or accounts lost, goods returned, negative reports in the trade press. If you suspect your company may be contemplating cutbacks, don't waste time on denial, worrying, gossiping, or complaining. Take action instead. Update your CV, register with a recruitment agency that specializes in your industry, and start checking out job ads in the paper. Maybe you'll be able to find a new (and even better) job before the axe falls.

If your redundancy comes as a total shock, take the following steps. Telephone all your contacts in the industry quickly. Ask about job prospects in their companies, and e-mail your CV to them and to their companies' human resource departments. Make getting that next job a full-time task and put all your energy into it, because the longer you remain unemployed the more people will get the impression (however unfairly) that there's something wrong with you. If necessary, accept a part-time or temporary job. It will be a source of needed income, and with luck it may turn into a full-time opportunity.

At the same time, take steps to shore up your financial situation. Cut luxuries from your budget. Be honest about your situation with your partner and children (if any), and enlist their support in economizing. Also be aware that the psychological impact of keeping these things to yourself can be highly damaging. Contact the Department for Work and Pensions to claim Jobseeker's Allowance, and phone your local council to see if you're entitled to housing benefit.

If you think you were unfairly dismissed, or that the pay-off you were offered wasn't enough, you can seek advice from your local Citizen's Advice or a lawyer who specializes in employment. However, don't waste too much energy on lawsuits or dreams of revenge.

Unable to Work

If you're ill or injured, your first priority is to get appropriate medical treatment. You will need a doctor's note (sometimes called a 'sick note') if you're unable to return to work after seven consecutive days off (including weekends and Bank Holidays). These will be replaced by 'fit notes' from 2010, telling you what you can do and how to get back to work. Employees are entitled to Statutory Sick Pay,

currently £79.15 per week, for twenty-eight weeks, as long as they made the normal National Insurance contributions. Many employers however are more generous. If you're self-employed, you can claim incapacity benefits if you have paid National Insurance. It is currently set at £67.75 a week. That's not enough for most people to live on, so I hope you took my advice and got income protection insurance that will kick in after sixty or ninety days, by which time your savings could be dwindling.

If you're an employee and are still too sick to return to work after you've had your twenty-eight weeks of Statutory Sick Pay, you can claim incapacity benefit. It may not be much, but in an emergency even a small amount like this can be useful.

Make sure you keep up your National Insurance contributions to maintain your entitlement to all kinds of benefits, including your state pension. If you've fallen behind due to a period when you weren't working (for example, if you took time off to have a baby), then contact the Contributions Office and make up the shortfall (see page 243).

Central Heating Boiler Meltdown

The most common time for your home heating system to break down is when you need it most: in the depths of winter. Unless you want to spend the next few weeks wearing several layers of clothing and washing in ice-cold water, you'll have to move fast when a problem occurs. Find a central heating engineer to diagnose the problem. Ask around for personal recommendations or find one via a website that carries consumer recommendations. Make sure you use one who is on the Gas Safe Register for gas installations.

If you need a new boiler, it could cost you £1,000 or more. You should have enough in your savings account to pay for it. If not, take out the lowest-cost loan you can find and arrange to pay it back quickly, making the highest monthly repayments you can manage.

The boiler manufacturer or local gas supplier may offer you a maintenance contract, whereby they come to fix it if there is any trouble and give it an annual service. You don't need this with a brand-new boiler, which is covered under guarantee. But when the guarantee period ends, a maintenance contract costing £10 to £15 a month can be a good deal. Of course, read the small print and make sure that the contract covers parts as well as labour.

House Fire

People sometimes ask the question, 'If your house was on fire and you could only save one thing, what would you save?' The right answer is 'Nothing!' If there's a fire in your home, get all the people outside, and then call the fire brigade. Don't even stop to pick up handbags, wallets, jewellery, or other valuables. Lives have been lost that way.

If you're lucky, the fire brigade will be able to put the fire out reasonably quickly, perhaps limiting the damage to one or two rooms. Unfortunately, smoke and water can cause almost as much devastation as flames. Wait until you are given the all-clear, then go back in and see what can be salvaged. In a worst-case scenario, where you've lost everything, including all your cards and financial records, you may have to pay a visit to your local bank branch to get some cash and order replacement cards.

If you've forgotten the name of your insurance company, your bank will be able to find this out by searching for the direct debit in your current account. If you are a homeowner, you will need to contact both your buildings and contents insurers, who will send a loss adjustor to have a look at the damage as soon as possible. If you are renting, then contact the landlord as well as your contents insurer.

So long as you were fully covered, your insurance carrier will normally offer you alternative accommodation until your home is habitable again. Contents insurers operate in various ways, but many companies will try to replace the goods that were destroyed. In some cases you may have to replace them out of your own pocket and then claim the money back with receipts attached to a claim form. Consult the insurance companies at each step along the way and make sure you follow their procedures exactly.

Car Accident

If you are involved in a car accident, you must stop if you damage another vehicle or property, or injure a person or animal. If necessary, call an ambulance. You must also report the accident to the police. Even if you don't require emergency medical treatment, you should record any injuries you incur in case you need to claim compensation in the future.

If no one is injured but the cars are damaged, make a note of the other driver's registration number, name, address, and insurance company. Take down the contact details of any witnesses as well. If you have a mobile phone or camera with you, take some photos of the accident scene.

If your damaged car is obstructing traffic, move it out of the way. If it is too badly damaged to be driven, call the police or the highways agency if the accident happened on a motorway. If you are not blocking traffic, call your insurance company, a breakdown service, or a local garage to tow it away.

If you have only third-party insurance and the accident was your fault, you will have to pay for repairs to your own car. Shop around and choose the best quote. If you have comprehensive insurance or you think it was the other driver's fault, wait for your insurance company's approval before going ahead with repairs. You may have to pay for them and claim back the cost later. Many insurers will arrange for the repairs to be carried out by an approved garage, which means the insurer pays and repairs are often guaranteed.

Identity Theft

One of the first signs that you are a victim of this increasingly common crime is when unexplained items turn up on your credit card bill or bank statement. Phone the bank or credit card company immediately to find out what they are. Keep a record of all the conversations and copies of letters or emails. Some banks insist you close your account, others will advise you to keep them open (with a block or monitor on transactions).

In England and Wales, it is up to the bank – not you – to report the crime to the police. In Scotland you can still report ID fraud to the police. Contact the three credit reference agencies – Equifax, Experian, and Callcredit (see page 244) – to find out if any other accounts have been opened in your name.

Try to figure out when your identification details and account numbers could have been stolen. This may help give you an idea of how much information the thief has. Did you put statements, bills, or financial correspondence in the rubbish, without shredding them? Could someone else have access to your post? Did a stranger stand very close to you at a cash machine recently? Are any cards missing? Where are your passport and driving licence?

You can also buy protective registration from CIFAS, which means your details are added to a register as having been a victim of fraud. Lenders will make additional checks before they grant credit, which should stop you from becoming a victim of fraud for a second time.

Close any accounts that may have been compromised and get replacement cards with new account numbers. When choosing new security passwords and PIN numbers, don't pick obvious ones like your mother's maiden name or your date of birth. Experts advise that nearly random combinations of letters and numbers provide the highest level of security.

Unfortunately, if the thief got enough information to open new accounts in your name, your nightmare may not yet be over. In the worst cases, it can take years to clean up your credit reports and financial information to where they were before. Whatever you do, stand firm and don't pay any bills that aren't rightfully yours. Keep records of every conversation and copies of all correspondence you have with the banks and companies involved. And keep checking your new account statements and your credit reference file like a hawk.

Separation

If you and your partner decide to separate after a marriage or a long relationship during which your financial affairs have become intertwined, the way you disentangle them is very important. The whole process will be far easier if you have remained informed about your household finances over the years. If your partner always dealt with the money matters, you may now be facing a very steep learning curve.

The first step is to list all the assets and liabilities you hold between you, checking recent statements to make sure your figures are completely up to date. Discuss whether you need legal or financial advice to split them up.

If you have previously put your earnings into a joint account, open a new one in your name only. Decide how to split the money in any joint bank or building society accounts, then close those accounts. (If you don't do this, you could be held liable for any debts your partner runs up in those accounts.) If your breakup is not amicable, you may have to ask the bank to freeze the account. Generally both signatures are needed to close a joint account, although sometimes only one is needed to freeze it.

As a newly single person, you will probably have to live with a new, more restrictive budget. Make a new monthly budget using the form on pages 21–2 to figure out how much you need to live on. This will give you a fair idea of the kind of settlement you may need to seek in any divorce proceeding.

Check through all your insurance needs, since you may have had joint policies with your partner. When time permits, review your personal retirement planning to see whether the pension you are building is sufficient. If one spouse has a much larger pension, it can be divided at the time of divorce. However, you will need specific financial advice on this matter.

SCOUNDRELS AND SCAMS

Don't assume that only people who are greedy or stupid fall for scams. Today, many scammers are well dressed and slick; some boast nice offices, impressive literature, and glitzy websites. Figures from the Office of Fair Trading show that over 3 million adults fall for scams every year, losing £3.5 billion among them. Separate research by the same organisation showed that some knowledge of investments actually made people more likely to fall for the scams. Here are some well-known scams:

- Pyramid schemes (a.k.a. chain-letter schemes), where you send cash to names at the top of a list in order to get your name added to the bottom. You may even know people who've made money from them, because they tend to circulate within small communities as people pass them on to their friends. Such schemes work only as long as willing victims continue to climb on at the bottom rung. Eventually, the whole thing collapses. In the end, 88 per cent of the people who put money into such schemes are losers – it's mathematically provable!
- Unsolicited mailshots that tell you you've won fabulous prizes. A telltale sign that this is a scam: the sponsors of the 'contest' ask for your bank account or credit card details before you can claim your prize. Others ask you to send a cheque as a registration fee. A similar scam targets mobile phones, telling you you've won a prize and have to call a premium-rate number to claim it. Don't! The call will cost a fortune, and the prize will be subject to so many conditions you'll never be able to use it.
- The 'West African fortune' scam. Victims are approached by letter or e-mail claiming that due to some emergency in an African country large sums of money are trapped in a special account there, whose owner (often described as a prince, former prime minister, or other dignitary) needs the help of a UK citizen to get it out. You are offered a proportion of the money in exchange for your help. The steps you have to take are seemingly painless, and the money is due to arrive in your account when you get a call to say that a bribe is needed to get some state official to release the funds. You give them the bribe money – and they're never heard of again.
- 'Boiler room' scams where a bogus stockbroker, usually based overseas, contacts you and tries to sell you shares in a sure-fire winner. Previously, scammers often tried to sell shares in oil companies, but with climate change becoming more of

an issue, they have a new twist: shares in green businesses and climate-friendly companies.

The average amount lost by victims is £20,000, although the highest boiler room loss is a staggering £1.2 million. Many of those who've fallen for this scam have been people with investment experience but, post credit-crunch, scammers are now targeting younger, less-experienced victims.

Never buy shares offered to you in this way, no matter how good the deal sounds. Sometimes the companies recommended by these rogue brokers exist, but they never have the investment potential you're promised. Hang up the phone and report the scam.

If you suspect you've been scammed or are being targeted for a scam, check the Consumer Direct website (www.consumerdirect.gov.uk/watch_out/Commonscams/). It describes a long list of known scams, from miracle lotions to homeworking scams, bogus holidays to clairvoyants to on-line dating scams. There is an equally long list of safeguards and checks you should apply before signing up to any deal.

GUIDELINE: Never provide anyone with financial or other personal information until you have established whether the company they represent is legitimate. Use common sense and contact Consumer Direct if you aren't sure about the company you are dealing with. Talk to friends and family about what you're being offered. Many scammers tell you not to talk about your 'good fortune' to your nearest and dearest. Never, ever part with money under pressure and seek advice from a financial adviser, accountant, or solicitor before parting with any substantial sum.

DON'T TAKE IT LYING DOWN

British people aren't very good at complaining. Perhaps it's due to the famous British reserve, their instinctive politeness, or the 'stiff-upper-lip' mentality that enabled them to persevere through the hard times of the twentieth century. All are admirable traits, but being able to complain effectively when it's appropriate is good for your self-esteem as well as your bank balance.

This is especially true when it comes to purchases of financial products: investments, insurance policies, annuities, bank accounts, and loans.

If you think you were misled when you bought a financial product, start by re-reading all the paperwork. The contract, sales brochure, or other document should spell out the risks involved.

You have valid grounds for complaint if you were sold a product that was not suitable; such as, if you were led to believe that an investment was risk-free and you later lost money on it. For example, tens of thousands of people were sold payment protection insurance (PPI) that they didn't want, didn't need or couldn't claim on. PPI should pay the installments of your loans or credit cards – normally the minimum payments for credit cards – during the time you cannot work due to illness or because you have lost your job. However, many of these policies have exclusions which mean some people find it impossible to make a claim. Some were sold PPI policies without being told of the exclusions, while others had the cost added to their loan without their knowledge. The Financial Services

Authority has fined over 20 companies for mis-selling this insurance.

Here's how to complain about a possibly fraudulent or misleading financial product. Begin by writing to the person who sold you the product. Mark the letter 'Formal Complaint'. Outline your grievance and, if possible, indicate how much you think you've lost as a result. If you

don't get the response you want, write to the managing director at company headquarters. Most companies have a complaints procedure, which may resolve your problem fairly.

If the company's response isn't what you think it ought to be, don't give up. You may be able to complain to the Financial Ombudsman Service. A useful leaflet called the *Guide to Making a Complaint* is published by the industry watchdog, the FSA. Request it on-line at moneymadeclear.fsa.gov.uk or by phone on 0300 500 5000). You can also get free telephone advice from their well-informed advisers.

Of course, not every financial loss creates a right to complain. For example, if you were advised to put your money into a particular share investment or unit trust in 2006 or 2007, you may find that the sharp stock market decline that followed reduced the value of your investment substantially. However, this is not your adviser's fault – provided, of course, that you were notified about the risks that are always involved in share investing.

GUIDELINE: If you believe you've been misled or defrauded when purchasing a financial product, don't hesitate to complain. You can help yourself by taking the time to educate yourself about the potential risks and rewards *before* making any investment or financial decision; however don't blame yourself if you were sold an unsuitable product. Sometimes even the best prepared investor can be a victim of mis-selling.

NO ILL WILL

Families are increasingly complicated nowadays, with many people having second and third marriages, step-children, half-brothers and -sisters, step-uncles, and quarter cousins. There aren't even names for some of the new relationships in which we find ourselves. So how can any one-size-fits-all law apply fairly to every single family in the land? But that's precisely the kind of law that governs the inheritance of money and property when someone dies *intestate* – that is, without making a will. And to make things more complicated, Scotland has different rules from the rest of the UK.

Consider the following scenarios. Can you predict who would inherit?

Q A husband dies leaving a £700,000 estate, of which the most valuable asset is the marital home. He has no children, and his parents are dead, but he has one sister with whom he hasn't been in contact for years. Will his widow get his entire estate?

A No. In England and Wales, the estranged sister can claim £125,000 from the estate, even if this forces the widow to sell the family home to release the money. In Scotland, the widow has prior rights. This means, if there are no children, that she is entitled to the first £300,000 of her husband's interest in the house, up to the first £24,000 of assets such as furniture, and up to £75,000 of cash. What is left is shared under 'legal rights' in a specified order.

Q **A man sets up house with a woman who has a very young child from an earlier marriage. He raises the child as his own, and they have another child together, but he and the woman never marry, although they live together for forty years. Who gets his money when he dies?**

A His biological child would have the automatic claim. If the house was owned as joint tenants, his partner would inherit his share. Otherwise, his partner would have to make a claim under the Inheritance Act, so long as they lived in England or Wales. In Scotland she might be able to use the Family Law Act to make a claim.

Q **A childless couple have lived together for thirty years when Partner A dies. Partner B had always assumed that the house belonged to both of them, but when the deed is examined, it turns out that the house was owned solely by Partner A who has no brothers and sisters. Who inherits the house?**

A Partner A's parents, although a claim might be possible under the Inheritance Act or Family Law Act as above.

As these examples illustrate, the inheritance laws are a maze of complications. The only thing you can be sure of is that, if you die intestate, there's a strong possibility that your money will not go to the people you want to have it.

Anticipating the reality of death doesn't make the event happen one minute earlier! It does, however, make coping with death easier for your loved ones. The emotional impact of death is bad enough without discovering that you have to wade through a legal and financial minefield. When someone dies intestate, it can take far longer for his or her money to be released to the family. Don't you want to spare your nearest and dearest all that trouble and trauma?

Making a will can also help you to avoid or minimize inheritance tax. The current threshold is £325,000; the value of your estate above that level is taxable at a 40 per cent rate. (Nowadays the value of a family home can easily take estates over that limit.) Married couples and those in a civil partnership can effectively double this allowance of £325,000 (giving a total of £650,000).

GUIDELINE: If you have a spouse or partner, children, a home or business, or any people or causes that you want to care for after death, you need a will. Don't put it off. Make a will now so that your loved ones will remember you fondly rather than regretting your lack of foresight.

PLANNING FOR THE GREAT BEYOND

Writing a will is just one part of the process of preparing for your demise. Here's a checklist that will make it easier for you to tackle the job.

1. There are three ways to make a will. You can buy a DIY form from a stationery shop, consult with a company that specializes in wills, or hire a solicitor. I recommend either using solicitor or a member of the Institute of Professional Willwriters. A solicitor may be able to give you additional advice and act as your *executor* if you wish (see below). Of course, they will also ensure that your will is legally binding, which it might not be if you make an unknown error in the DIY kind. Using a solicitor won't be prohibitively expensive if you plan thoughtfully in advance.

2. Take a list of all your main assets to the solicitor's office. (You could use the one you made up on page 24 of this book.) Decide who should get what. List any special bequests: for example, your Elvis albums to your old motorcycle chum, your clothes to Oxfam, and your pearl necklace to a favourite niece. (If there are dozens of special bequests, you can make this a separate list rather than part of the will itself. This way you can change the list without having to write a new will.) Then decide who should get whatever is left after all specified assets have been distributed.

3. Choose an executor, who will be responsible for making sure all your wishes are carried out. You can select a family member (including a beneficiary in the will), a trusted friend, or a solicitor. Ask how much he/she charges. It's also polite to check beforehand that they don't mind being named your executor. It's prudent to name a second executor who will handle the job if the first executor dies before you, or at the same time.

4. If you have children under the age of eighteen, your will should state who you would want to look after them if you die before they are grown up. Once again, it's common sense to ask the person's consent before nominating them. You may also choose to nominate an animal-loving guardian for any pets you might leave behind.

5. When specifying the division of financial assets, use percentages rather than pound amounts, so your bequests will remain appropriate no matter how your investments may change in value. Rather than '£10,000 to my sister Jane,' leave her 'one-third of my share investment portfolio'.

6. In a separate document, you can describe what you want to happen to your body: cremation, burial, and if burial, where? Make sure your loved ones know about this or you could end up spending eternity with the wrong ex-spouse. If you have preferences regarding the funeral ceremony, list them here.

7. You should also draw up a Lasting Power of Attorney (LPA) which sets out who will take over your financial and/or welfare decisions should you become incapable of doing so. Without such a

document, your next of kin would have to get the court to appoint someone and you wouldn't have any say in who it is.

8. Get two signatories to witness your will (you don't have to show them what's in it), then keep copies in a safe place. For example, you might keep one copy in a filing cabinet at home and one in your solicitor's office. Make sure your executors know where it is, so they don't need to turn the house upside down after you die.

9. If you have property worth more than £325,000, talk with a knowledgeable accountant, financial adviser, or solicitor about how to minimize inheritance tax. An estate planning expert can review the rules with you and help you devise a strategy that will work.

10. Review your will whenever circumstances change: if you get married or divorced, if you have children or grandchildren, if the people you have named as heirs die before you, or if your financial status changes significantly. Note that previous wills become invalid if you marry after making them (except in Scotland). You can make revisions to former wills, but if you decide to make a new one be sure to specify that it 'revokes all others'.

GUIDELINE: Preparing for your death may sound like a lot of work, and if your financial status is complicated, it can be. But it's a lot less work than your heirs will face if you die without proper planning.

KEEPING YOURSELF AND YOUR MONEY ON TRACK

In the chapters you've read so far, you've learned about dozens of important strategies for managing, keeping, spending, and growing your money. Now it's time to assemble all the pieces into a coherent, workable plan that can enhance your financial prospects for life. Consider who you are – your personality and attitude towards money – your needs and obligations, and your dreams for the future. Then start working towards your goals. I know you can do it – so why not begin today?

THE QUEST FOR FINANCIAL CONTENTMENT

As you pursue your financial dreams, you'll want to monitor where you are in relation to your goals. This includes checking how much money you've accumulated relative to the amount you need for buying a home, opening a business, educating your children, retiring from work, and any other goals you've set. Monitoring the growth of your bank account in this way is a straightforward mathematical process.

There's a second kind of self-monitoring that's more subtle but equally important. It involves evaluating your *emotional* state in regard to money. Ask yourself questions like these:

- Is my life pretty good now, or could it get better?
- When I think about my financial future, do I feel happy or anxious?
- Am I happy with the path I am on, or should I change it?
- What can I do to give myself and those I love a greater sense of satisfaction *today*, without losing the motivation to continue striving towards *tomorrow's* long-term objectives?

Take some time to reflect on your answers to these questions. People who achieve their goals in life (including those beyond finances) find the right balance between day-to-day contentment and the desire to strive, to grow, to achieve. What's the proper balance? It's different for each person.

For most people, achieving the ideal balance will probably mean using the information in this book to tweak some habits or plans. For some, it may require major life changes. The point here is best summarized in three verbs: *Focus. Decide. Act.*

You may find you want to downsize your financial expectations, opting for both a more simple, less pressured working life and a richer day-to-day personal life. Others may choose to continue to strive for a high level of professional and financial achievement, partly because the work is stimulating and rewarding, partly because success produces a sense of pride and independence. For still others, work may be simply a means to an end, such as a life of leisure on a golf course, at an ashram, in holiday spots around the world, or simply in your garden. There are no choices that are absolutely right or wrong – only choices that are right or wrong *for you*.

Statistics show that most people are at their wealthiest as they approach fifty. How does this fact make you feel? If you are in your twenties or early thirties, you still have time to reach this apex; now is a good time to be planning how you will achieve this height and what you will do to preserve some of that wealth for your elder years. If you are already near or over fifty and are disappointed with the level of wealth you've achieved, consider this your wake-up call. It's never too late to improve your future. But the longer you wait, the greater the sacrifices that will be required.

No matter what your age, the key to controlling your money today and building long-term financial security tomorrow is to develop and follow an individual plan that is:

- **Sustainable** – a plan you can stick to through life's inevitable twists and turns.
- **Satisfying** – a plan that provides the pleasure you need to stay motivated.
- **Self-perpetuating** – a plan that helps you build a nest egg that will grow on its own, ultimately supporting you in an enjoyable and rewarding lifestyle.

Periodic check-ups are necessary to make sure your plan is still on the right track. Your life, financial situation, or goals may have changed. Your normal discipline may have begun to drift. The only way to know if your plans are on course is to check them yourself. Don't abdicate this responsibility. And be totally honest with yourself during the check-ups.

GUIDELINE: Avoid letting envy, comparison, and peer pressure make you unhappy with your financial plans. Know what *you* require to feel financially secure and content, and focus on that goal.

PERIODIC ACTIVITIES AND REVIEWS

Once you've got your finances in order and your long-term plan in place, it should take about an hour a week – a little more at first – to monitor and maintain it. Choose a time each week when you know you'll have the quiet and concentration to get the task finished in one sitting. Don't break it apart – a little now, a little later – because it's too easy to get distracted or to justify putting it off until another time.

There are other self-evaluation tasks that need to be completed monthly, quarterly, and annually. Just like periodic check-ups for your car and your body, you need to monitor the health of your finances. Remember: If you expect your money to take care of you, you must take care of it.

Once a Week

- As you make purchases or withdraw money from cash machines during the week, put all the receipts in one place – an envelope, a folder, a basket. (Personally, I like a clear glass vase because you can see the accumulation over the course of the week. The more papers you see, the more you're spending.) During your once-a-week check-up, total what you've spent in each area of your budget (see pages 21–2). If you've overspent in any category, decide where you can make cutbacks during the upcoming week to get yourself back on track.

- As bills arrive, check them to make sure the amount looks right. Then stack them up by due date. Once a week, pull out the bills and pay the ones that are due. Pay on time to avoid late fees and damage to your credit rating. You can simplify your life by paying by direct debit. Some companies offer you a discount on your bills for doing so.
- If you are considering buying shares or already own some, check the internet or financial pages at least once a week. Review what has happened to the price of any shares you own or are interested in, and see what news stories have affected them.

Once a Month

- Reconcile your debit and credit card receipts and cheque book stubs and cash machine receipts with your bank statements and credit card bills. Tick every item to catch any misplaced cheques, wrong amounts, double charges, or incorrect fees. Also keep an eye out for fraudulent activity or identity theft. Ignoring your bank statement can cost you a lot more than just lost interest and overdraft charges. If you don't catch these errors or mistakes, then no one will.
- If you are self-employed, make your monthly National Insurance payment. Also set aside money for tax and VAT (if applicable), preferably in a separate bank account. Most people find it easier to put a little away each month than to come up with one large sum when the quarterly VAT and twice-yearly tax payments are due. Also, if you leave the money in your current account, you might be tempted to spend some or all of it.
- When you total your monthly spending in each category, transfer any money you haven't spent into a savings account. If you've come in under budget in two or more categories, consider buying yourself a treat with part of the money you saved.
- If any of your shares are giving you cause for concern, consider whether it's time to sell them. But don't sell just because the price is down; review the guidelines provided in this book (see pages 132–4).

Once a Quarter

- If you have a financial adviser, send them and email or ring them to discuss your finances. Use this to get a sense of what he or she thinks of the current economy and what you can expect for the rest of the year. But do your own homework first, as noted in the rest of this section.
- Check the balance in your savings account. Make sure that interest has been added correctly and deposits have been credited. Check on-line comparison sites to see whether you could be getting a higher interest rate elsewhere. If so, consider transferring your money (provided you are not in a thirty-, sixty-, or ninety-day lock-in period). Have a look at the best deals in current accounts and credit cards and consider whether it would be worth changing those as well.
- Call your pension companies and get a statement of the total saved. If your plans aren't growing as fast as you need them to, confer with your financial adviser about other actions you can take if the trend continues.
- Review your shareholdings. Do they still have the growth potential that made you invest in them initially? Consider selling if they are close to any maximum price limit you may have set. If they have declined in price, yet seem due for an upswing, consider buying additional shares.
- Is the car going to need new tyres? Is your freezer on its last legs? Is holiday time coming around again? Plan and budget for any major purchases you will need to make in the next quarter, and decide about clothing purchases for the coming season. Try to save up the money to cover new purchases rather than borrowing it.

Once a Year

- Look at the best deals in mortgages in your weekend paper, and consider refinancing if there are significant savings to be had (after weighing transaction costs and possible prepayment penalties, of course).
- If you have an endowment or ISA mortgage, check whether your investments seem to be on track to pay off the amount of the capital sum you need them to cover. If not, consider switching part of your interest-only mortgage to repayment.
- Check the current values of all your investments: cash, bonds, shares, and unit trusts or funds. Are they growing the way you need them to in order to meet your future goals? If not, consider changing the investment mix or increasing the amount you save so as to boost the growth of your nest egg.

GUIDELINE: Don't be one of the 12 per cent of people in the UK who don't check their bank statements, or the 25 per cent who have no idea how much they owe on credit cards or store cards. How can you take control of your money when your head is in the sand? Ignorance may be bliss – but in today's world it can also be costly.

WRITE YOUR OWN
ANNUAL REPORT

Once a year, either in January or around the time you fill in your tax return (if you complete one), sit down and write a report assessing how you handled your finances during the past twelve months. It's your opportunity to look back with 20/20 hindsight at what you did well and did poorly. The process can be surprisingly satisfying and revealing.

Be honest and dispassionate. Don't do what large companies tend to do when they publish their annual reports: put a favourable spin on every situation, blame failures on extraneous forces, and sidestep difficult issues. Instead, use the report to:

- Evaluate your successes and failures during the past year.
- Determine where you wasted or misused money.
- Chart your progress towards your goals.
- Enumerate the changes you want to make for the coming year.
- Set specific goals and challenges for the next year.

Actually putting pen to paper or your fingers to the keyboard is an essential part of the process. By capturing your actions in black and white, you'll develop objectivity and acquire the needed insights about yourself that will help you to take increasing control of yourself and your money. Here are some items to cover in your report.

- Your income this year compared with your income last year.
- Any changes in your financial situation.
- The amount of money you saved or invested this year compared to last year.
- The current value of your assets, including savings and investments.
- The current amount of your liabilities: mortgage remaining, credit card debt, student loans, etc. Did they increase or decrease this year compared to last year?
- The amount of short-term debt you are carrying relative to your liquid assets.
- Your current net worth. Calculate this by subtracting your total liabilities (all debts including the amount of your outstanding mortgage) from your total assets (including the reasonable market value of your property). Is this number higher or lower than past years? Is there an upward trend or a downward trend?
- The percentage of your total income spent in the key categories of your budget. Where did you overspend relative to your budget? Why?
- The best financial decision you made during the year.
- The worst financial decision you made during the year.
- The financial skills at which you were strongest and weakest.
- The specific changes you need to make in yourself and your budget next year. (Don't defeat yourself by setting more changes than you can effectively make.)
- Your specific goals for next year. (List just three to five goals per year. This way you will remember them and, hopefully, accomplish them.)

Conclude your report with a three-paragraph evaluation of yourself and your financial situation and a clearly stated personal resolution for the future. Is your financial situation improving or deteriorating? Is there any opportunity for it to get better in the coming year? You should be able to see where you are vulnerable, as well as where you are healthy.

Don't beat yourself up about mistakes you've made. But do learn something from them and, most important, carry that wisdom and insight into your future. After all, it is the future that you can change.

GUIDELINE: Everyone makes mistakes, in financial matters as in every area of life. But at the end of each year, you want to have taken more positive actions than negative. The net result should be a positive increase in your overall wealth – and your wisdom.

DON'T LOSE YOUR BALANCE

Each year as you write your Annual Report, you can re-evaluate where you are in the Great Scheme of Things and plan any changes that need to be made for the next stage of life.

Remember the asset allocation chart on page 116? As time passes, the value of your investments in each of these asset groups will rise and fall, inevitably changing percentages in your portfolio. Monitor these changes and take the appropriate remedial steps by *rebalancing your portfolio* periodically – preferably once a year.

For example, suppose at the beginning of the year you decided to hold 40 per cent of your portfolio in shares and 60 per cent in bonds and other assets. But if the shares of specific companies that you own have risen significantly in value since then, it might mean that you now have 55 per cent of your assets in shares. In that case, it would make sense to sell some or all of those shares to capture those gains and reinvest the profits in the more stable bonds in your portfolio. In this way, you restore the portfolio to the 40:60 allocation you initially set.

Remember that, as the date approaches when you will need money to pay for long-term goals (such as education or retirement), you will want gradually to change your asset allocation mix. For example, about five years before you need the money to pay your first child's university fees, you might start to 'rotate' your investments out of higher-risk items (such as shares) and into safer assets like cash or bonds. Don't make these changes all at one time. Move

your money a little at a time, taking advantage of different market conditions.

In the same vein, if you're planning to retire at the age of sixty-five, you should gradually start to rotate towards cash and bonds in your early or mid-fifties, rather than crossing your fingers that the market conditions will be favourable ten years later.

When you want to sell shares, select those that you judge are closest to their peak value, or those that are dropping and seem unlikely to recover any time soon. Remember to set aside any capital gains tax that will be payable. Reinvest in bonds, choosing ones that offer income if you need it. You can also reduce the risk and volatility in your portfolio by shifting from small company shares to blue chips.

You may find that your risk tolerance changes as you get older. From time to time, reconsider how much you could afford to lose. You should be prepared, financially and psychologically, to forfeit 30 per cent (this is a general benchmark) of any money you invest in the stock market (in the event of a sudden market downturn like the one in 2008/2009).

Getting older needn't be all about moving your money into totally safe positions. As you become more experienced at share investing and have a realistic understanding of risk tolerance, you may decide to put more money into the stock market. You could have lots of spare cash because the kids have left home and the mortgage is paid off, or because you receive an inheritance or windfall. So long as your pension plans are secure and you can afford to lose the money without diminishing your lifestyle, you might consider increasing the amount of money you invest in stocks. Always keep your holdings diversified across sectors, companies, and countries.

Do you want to set up trusts to help your children avoid inheritance tax after your death? Get legal advice, because the chancellor is cutting back on these loopholes at every opportunity. Alternatively, you may decide to join the SKI club (short for 'Spend the Kids' Inheritance') and enjoy the fruits of all your years of toil – but don't forget to leave provision in case you need nursing-home care at some stage.

GUIDELINE: Balance is a dynamic aspect of our lives. As the various forces – family, career, health, money – change, as they inevitably will, you may find yourself drifting or being blown off the path you set for yourself. Once a year take the time to look at your situation and make the necessary corrections to keep you on course.

THE PRICE OF MENTAL FREEDOM

'The mass of men lead lives of quiet desperation,' wrote Henry David Thoreau, the American naturalist and philosopher. In the modern world, there are many triggers that can make us desperate, from fears of terrorism to AIDS. But few of these triggers are more powerful than money or the lack of it. Serious financial problems are leading causes of divorce, depression, even suicide.

In many cases, the aura of mystery and secrecy that surrounds money helps to make financial problems more severe than they need to be. People expect money to be magical, with transformative and life-fulfilling powers. And mystery surrounds money because no one really knows why some people manage to get and hold on to more of it than others.

Yet the truth is that good money management skills can be simple and straightforward for the majority of people. If you or I had the assets of Richard Branson or the reclusive Barclay brothers, our personal finances would be complicated. But handling average amounts of money well is largely a matter of common sense and a few basic ground rules.

If you have followed the advice in this book step by step, you should be well on your way to achieving a comfortable balance in your finances. Not everyone will get a kick out of managing money. I'm certainly not advocating that you become obsessed with checking share prices and saving every last penny in high-interest accounts. Once you've set up your financial plan, it should only take an hour a week to keep it balanced. The rest of your time is for living and enjoying the fruits of your labour.

If you have been chronically anxious about money in the past, try to visualize the following scenarios. They should all be possible once you've followed the advice in this book:

- Before your credit card bill arrives at the end of the month, you know how much it will be and you have the money in the bank to pay it in full.
- When your washing machine starts spewing water on to the kitchen floor, you have enough in a contingency fund to have it repaired or buy a new machine straight away.
- You know exactly how much your mortgage payment will be every month, and when the entire capital sum will be paid off.
- You have a pension plan in place that will provide you with a comfortable retirement income, and some investments that will let you enjoy a bit of travel and other treats in your old age.

Money buys you choices, while lack of money limits your options. With sufficient money, you can choose where you'll live, indulge in hobbies and leisure pursuits that you enjoy, take care of your children for as long as they need you to, and give generously to charities and causes you care about. It's no more – and no less – important than that.

GUIDELINE: Instead of expending energy worrying about your financial situation, divert the same energy into managing it wisely. More positive results are likely from thoughtful actions than from just thinking.

WHAT MONEY CAN'T BUY

You've just read a whole book about money: how to get it, keep it, use it, and make it grow. And I hope you'll follow the advice it teaches. But I also hope you'll keep money and its importance in perspective. After all, money and the material things it buys don't give meaning to life. For most people, true happiness comes from non-material things, such as:

- Spending quality time with family and loved ones.
- Writing, painting, playing music, or pursuing your own personal kind of creative fulfilment.
- Enjoying fresh air, beautiful countryside, mountains and oceans.
- Pursuing spiritual peace.
- Sharing laughter, jokes, and just having fun.
- Enjoying good health.
- Swimming, running, skiing, or other physical pursuits.
- Reading great books, looking at art, going to concerts.
- Meeting and getting to know new people.
- Experiencing meaningful work, hobbies, or relationships.

Which of these items are most important to you? What other activities belong on your list of life's greatest pleasures?

Now ask: How many hours do you spend on each item every week? Is it enough? Can you find more?

Yes, having money can make it easier to find the time for the joys of life. It can also bring you the peace of mind you need to put aside anxiety and open your heart and mind completely to the experiences of the moment. Thus, money is a vital tool in the pursuit of happiness. But never forget that it's only a tool, not the end in itself.

Never stop growing!

JUGGLING JARGON

APR Stands for Annual Percentage Rate, and indicates how much of a fee you pay to a lender for the privilege of borrowing money from them. A standard credit card APR could be between 16 and 18 per cent, meaning that if you leave a debt of £100 on a card for a year, you will owe approximately £116 or £118 respectively, at the end of the year.

Base rate In the UK, the Bank of England sets a base interest rate, which they increase or decrease when they think it's necessary for the well being of the economy. Interest rates at banks, building societies, and financial institutions generally track changes in the base rate, meaning your savings account might produce more or less interest or, if you've got a variable-rate mortgage, your monthly payment could go up or down.

Blue-chip shares Named after the highest value chip in a casino, these are shares in well-established, already successful companies. They are more secure than shares in new or smaller companies, and less likely to experience massive swings in value – although an incompetent new managing director or CEO can always tip the balance.

Bonds When you buy a bond, you are lending money in return for a set rate of interest and for a set period of time. The amount of interest you earn depends in part on the risk associated with the issuer. You can buy bonds issued by companies called 'corporate bonds' or by the government called 'gilts'. See also Premium bonds.

Capital Gains Tax (CGT) A tax charged by the government (currently at 18 per cent) on profits you make on shares, on selling a property that's not your primary residence, and on all sorts of other areas. The government sets an annual capital gains that you can make before you pay CGT (currently £10,100).

Consumer debt This is a blanket term for all debts taken out to purchase goods or services for your personal needs. In general, it covers credit and store card debt, hire purchase, mail-order catalogues, bank loans, and overdrafts, but not mortgages or student loans.

Dividends Your share of the company's after tax profits that its Board of Directors decide to pay out to share holders. Most companies pay twice a year and the amount you recieve is based on the number of shares you own.

Endowments A type of savings plan popular in the 1980s and early 1990s, and often linked to a mortgage and designed to pay off the debt at the end of the term. However, they were partly dependent on the stock market continuing to grow at the same high rates it was enjoying back then. And it didn't. And that's why thousands of people had to face the reality that their endowments wouldn't pay off their mortgages.

Equity 1) The difference between the value of a property and the unpaid amount of the mortgage. For example, if you have a house worth £200,000 and your mortgage is only £50,000, then you have equity of £150,000. However, if you have a mortgage of £250,000 for the same house, then you have £50,000 worth of negative equity. 2) A general term used for shares because they represent ownership in the company that issued them.

Extended warranties When a shop assistant tells you that you can pay an extra £50 a year to insure your new TV set against any breakdowns, this is an extended warranty. My advice? Just say 'no thanks'. The set will be under guarantee anyway for a set period, then if it breaks down after that it'll be cheaper paying for your own TV repairman.

FTSE Pronounced 'footsie', this stands for the Financial Times Stock Exchange. The Financial Times produce a range of indexes indicating share values, such as the FTSE 100 (Britain's top 100 companies) or the FTSE All Share (around 800 of Britain's largest public companies).

Gilts The name for bonds issued by the British government. When you buy a gilt, you are lending money to the government. The bonds have a variety of different terms, also called maturities. The sum you pay for gilts will vary, as will the interest you receive on the bond, but each gilt has a 'par value' of £100, which is what you will receive if you hold it until the term is up.

Group personal pension A collection of individual personal pensions run by a pension provider, to which both you and your employer contribute. There are limits to the amount you can contribute depending on your age. You will get a lump sum on retirement, part of which must be used to purchase an annuity to give you regular income for the rest of your life.

Hire purchase Also known as 'rent-to-buy', hire purchase was often used when people needed to make large purchases but didn't have the money up front. Interest rates are high, and if you miss a couple of payments early on, the goods can be confiscated and you lose all the money you've paid to date.

HLC (Higher Lending Charge) If you borrow more than a certain amount (often 85-90 per cent) of the value of your property you are likely to be asked to pay an HLC, which is a kind of insurance policy to protect the mortgage provider in the event that you are unable to keep up with your repayments. Not all lenders charge an HLC so try to find one that does not.

Inflation The rate at which the prices we pay for goods and services increase in a given period. For example, in 1976 a pint of beer cost 30p. It now costs around £2.75.

Inheritance tax If someone leaves an estate worth more than £325,000, then their heirs will have to pay inheritance tax on the excess – unless they have planned ahead to minimize taxes or to offset some of the tax liability while they were still alive.

In the UK, married couples (or those in a civil partnership) can effectively double the IHT allowance to £650,000.

ISA Acronym for individual savings accounts. ISAs are like a kind of magic wrapping paper in which you can wrap up cash or stocks and shares to make the gains tax-free. The maximum contribution you can make to an ISA each year is set by the government.

Life assurance An insurance policy that will provide for your dependants if you should die before the end of the term (for 'term insurance'); 'whole of life' insurance provides a lump sum for your heirs whenever you die.

Liquid Asset Cash or an asset that can be easily turned into cash (such as shares) at short notice. Property, art and antiques are 'illiquid', because they cannot be easily and quickly turned into cash if you had to sell them in a hurry.

National Savings and Investments A range of savings products backed by the Treasury, some of which are tax-free. You'll find leaflets about them in all major post offices.

Occupational pension scheme There are two kinds: a) final salary schemes, where your employer guarantees to pay you, for the rest of your life, a percentage of the salary you are earning when you retire. b) defined contribution schemes, which the employee and employer contribute to, and the lump sum you receive on retirement depends on how well investments in the plan have done.

Options A derivative investment product whereby you purchase the right to buy or sell shares, commodities or other securities at a set price in the future. The right to buy or sell expires on a given date.

Portfolio 1) The name for your collection of savings and investments, comprising cash, shares, bonds, and property. 2) The name for the pooled group of securities that comprise a unit trust or fund.

Premium bonds A type of national savings product, in which you are entered into a monthly prize draw with a chance of winning up to £1 million.

Repossession The taking back of property (or ther items, such as your car) if you fail to keep up with your mortgage repayments or default on a loan that is secured on your property. You are still liable for the money you owe, and you have nowhere to live.

Shares As the name implies, a security representing part ownership in the company that issues them to the public. Share holders have the right to vote and to receive dividends.

Spread betting A highly risky type of investment strategy where you bet on movements of the stock market. It is unsuitable for most investors.

Stakeholder pension A personal pension scheme that is open to all people, including those who don't work. It is a very flexible scheme with low charges.

Stamp duty A tax you have to pay the government on certain purchases, like property and shares.

Stock market Also called the Stock Exchange, it is the centralised facility where securities (stocks, bonds and derivatives) are traded by stockbrokers and market makers, according to strict rules.

Tracker funds A type of pooled investment product designed to follow the movement of a designated share index, such as the FTSE All Share.

Unit trusts A collection of securities, typically the shares and/or bonds of different companies, pooled together to achieve diversity. The theory is that even if one investment in a unit trust plummets in value, the others may hold their value.

DIRECTORY

Debt Counselling

Citizen's Advice – find your local branch in the phone book
Websites: www.citizensadvice.org.uk OR www.adviceguide.org.uk

Consumer Credit Counselling Service (CCCS)
Tel: 0800 138 1111
E-mail: contactus@cccs.co.uk
Website: www.cccs.co.uk

National Debtline
Tel: 0808 808 4000
Website: www.nationaldebtline.co.uk

Community Legal Advice (for England and Wales only)
Tel: 0845 345 345
Website: www.communitylegaladvice.org.uk

Debtors' Anonymous
Tel: 020 7117 7533
Website: www.debtorsanonymous.org.uk

Legal Forms

OYEZ Straker
Tel: 0845 217 7565
Website: www.oyezformlink.co.uk

Claiming Benefits and State Pensions

Department for Work and Pensions

Benefit Enquiry line: 0800 882200 (only for people who are sick or disabled)

Websites: www.dwp.gov.uk OR www.jobcentreplus.gov.uk

To claim the basic state pension

Tel: 0800 731 7898 OR 0845 731 3233 for pension guides

Website: www.pensionguide.gov.uk

State Pension Forecasting Team, Future Pension Service

Room TB001

Tyneview Park

Whitley Road

Newcastle upon Tyne NE98 1BA

Tel: 0845 3000 168 (ask for form BR19)

Website: www.thepensionservice.gov.uk

Pensions Advisory Service

Tel: 0845 601 3923

Website: www.pensionsadvisoryservice.org.uk

National Insurance

Tel: 0845 302 1479

Website: www.hmrc.gov.uk

Industry Watchdog

Financial Services Authority (FSA)
25 The North Colonnade
Canary Wharf
London EI4 5HS
Tel: 0300 500 5000
Websites: www.moneymadeclear.fsa.gov.uk OR www.fsa.gov.uk

Credit Reference Agencies

Experian Ltd
Consumer Help Service
PO Box 8000
Nottingham NG80 7WF
Tel: 0844 481 8000
Website: www.experian.co.uk

Equifax plc
Credit File Advice Centre
PO Box 1140
Bradford BDI 5US
Tel: 0870 010 0583
Website: www.equifax.co.uk

Callcredit
One Park Lane
Leeds
West Yorkshire
LS3I IEP
Tel: 0870 060 1414
Website: www.callcredit.co.uk

National Savings and Investments

Tel: 0845 964 5000 (lines open 24 hours a day, call costs may vary depending on telephone provider)
Website: www.nsandi.com

Buying, Selling, or Letting Property

Websites with useful advice

www.fish4homes.co.uk
www.globrix.com
www.mouseprice.com
www.primelocation.com
www.propertyfinder.com
www.rightmove.co.uk
www.vebra.com

The Association of Residential Letting Agents (ARLA)

Tel: 0192 649 6800
Website: www.arla.co.uk

Shelter

Tel: 0808 800 4444
Website: www.shelter.org.uk

Advice on Unit Trusts and Funds

General information

The Investment Management Association (IMA)

Tel: 020 7269 4639
Website: www.investmentuk.org

Websites that compare funds

www.morningstar.co.uk OR www.trustnet.com

The Financial Times

Website: www.ft.com/funds

To Find an Independent Financial Adviser (IFA)

Unbiased.co.uk
(a website provided by IFA Promotions will give you contact details for independent financial advisers)

Institute of Financial Planning
Tel: 0117 945 2470
Website: www.financialplanning.org.uk

The Personal Finance Society
Website: www.findanadviser.org

Insurance Brokers

British Insurance Brokers' Association
Tel: 0870 950 1790
Website: www.biba.org.uk

Advice on ISAs

ISA helpline
Tel: 0845 604 1701
Website: www.hmrc.gov.uk/isa

Advice on Shares and Bonds

Website with specific company info:
www.companyrefs.com

Association of Private Client Investment Managers and Stockbrokers (APCIMS)
Tel: 020 7448 7100
Website: www.apcims.co.uk

GILTS
UK Debt Management Office
Tel: 0845 357 6500 (for copies of 'A private investors' guide to gilts').
Website: www.dmo.gov.uk

On-line Share Dealing (these may change frequently)
www.etrade.co.uk
www.fastrade.co.uk
www.halifax.co.uk/sharedealing
www.idealing.com
www.mybroker.com
www.selftrade.co.uk
www.share.com
www.stockbrokers.barclays.co.uk
www.stocktrade.co.uk
www.tdwaterhouse.co.uk

Price Comparison Sites
www.beatthatquote.com
www.confused.com
www.comparethemarket.com
www.gocompare.com
www.moneyfacts.co.uk
www.moneynet.co.uk
www.moneysupermarket.com
www.uswitch.com

Shopping Robots
www.pricerunner.co.uk
www.kelkoo.co.uk
www.ciao.co.uk
www.uk.shopping.com
www.buycentral.co.uk
www.smartshopping.co.uk

Energy Bills

Energy Saving Trust
Tel: 0800 512 012
Website: www.energysavingtrust.org.uk

Price Comparisons

www.confused.com
www.energyhelpline.com
www.energylinx.co.uk
www.homeadvisoryservice.co.uk
www.moneysupermarket.com
www.saveonyourbills.co.uk
www.simplyswitch.com
www.switchwithwhich.co.uk
www.theenergyshop.com
www.ukpower.co.uk
www.unravelit.com
www.uswitch.com

Consumer Direct (deals with initial enquiries or complaints
about energy)
Tel: 0845 404 0506
Website: www.consumerdirect.gov.uk

The Energy Ombudsman
Tel: 0845 055 0760 OR 01925 530 263
Website: www.energy-ombudsman.org.uk

Central Heating

Gas Safe Register
Tel: 0800 111 999
Website: www.gassaferegister.co.uk

To find an engineer in your area, try:
www.centralheating.co.uk

Consumer Rights

Consumer Direct
Tel: 0845 404 0506
Website: www.consumerdirect.gov.uk

Consumer Focus
Website: www.consumerfocus.org.uk

Trading Standards
To find your local office, look at your local council's website, use the phone book or go to www.tradingstandards.gov.uk

Savings and Investment Safety Schemes

Financial Services Compensation Scheme
Tel: 020 7892 7300
Website: www.fscs.org.uk

Pensions Protection Fund
Tel: 0845 600 2541
Website: www.pensionsprotectionfund.org.uk

For Complaints About Financial Products

Financial Ombudsman Service
South Quay Plaza
183 Marsh Wall
London E14 9SR
Tel: 0300 123 9 123 OR 020 7964 0500
Website: www.financial-ombudsman.org.uk
E-Mail: complaint.info@financial-ombudsman.org.uk

FSA Consumer helpline: 0845 606 1234
Consumer Website: www.fsa.gov.uk/consumer
E-mail: consumerhelp@fsa.gov.uk

INDEX